THE ART OF MANAGING HUMAN POWER

A Simple Guide for People Management

R K SHANKAR

INDIA • SINGAPORE • MALAYSIA

Notion Press

Old No. 38, New No. 6
McNichols Road, Chetpet
Chennai - 600 031

First Published by Notion Press in 2018
Republished by Notion Press in 2019
Copyright © R K Shankar 2019
All Rights Reserved.

ISBN 978-1-64324-143-2

This book has been published with all efforts taken to make the material error-free after the consent of the author. However, the author and the publisher do not assume and hereby disclaim any liability to any party for any loss, damage, or disruption caused by errors or omissions, whether such errors or omissions result from negligence, accident, or any other cause.

While every effort has been made to avoid any mistake or omission, this publication is being sold on the condition and understanding that neither the author nor the publishers or printers would be liable in any manner to any person by reason of any mistake or omission in this publication or for any action taken or omitted to be taken or advice rendered or accepted on the basis of this work. For any defect in printing or binding the publishers will be liable only to replace the defective copy by another copy of this work then available.

I adore God and my parents for showing the path and direction which has enabled in fulfilling the cherished desire of my life.

*This book is dedicated to my beloved brother Shri. R K Narayanan,
Dr. Govindappa Venkataswamy, Dr. Amar Agarwal &
Dr. Smita Narasimhan.*

In memory of his benign grace & invaluable contribution for the total transformation of my early part of life & career.

(21st March 1934 – 24th March 1987)
My beloved brother Shri. R K Narayanan

Dr. Govindappa Venkataswamy one of the most eminent ophthalmologist and 1973 recipient of Padma shri award & the founder of Aravind Eye Hospitals gave vision for my both eyes which were affected by cataract by performing successful surgeries when I was only about 2 years old.

(01ᵗʰ October 1918 – 07ᵗʰ July 2006)

"Intelligence and capability are not enough. There must be a joy of doing something beautiful."

– Dr. Govindappa Venkataswamy

The first Edition of this book was released in his centenary year (2018) as a tribute to Him & he would remain a legend forever……

Incidentally, the year 2018 happened to be the centenary year for my beloved mother (27ᵗʰ January 1918 – 12ᵗʰ August 2001) as well…

I invoke their blessings always to lead a simple and blissful life.

Dr. Amar Agarwal (Chairman of Dr. Agarwal's Eye Hospital Ltd., Chennai) & Dr. Smita Narasimhan

They gave a new life & fresh look to my eyes by implanting therein glued Intraocular lens (IOL) in August 2012 (when I was 57 years old) thereby improved my vision and enabled me to get rid of my thick glasses. No wonder, my confidence levels have been enhanced since then. I would say, it is a miracle in my life & a great boon indeed.

Contents

Foreword	11
Preface to the New Edition	13
Prologue	15
Acknowledgements	17

Part – I

Chapter-1	Beyond Systems to People – an Overview of HRD	21
Chapter-2	Managing Human Power for Personal Effectiveness	29
Chapter-3	Knowledge Process Management	38
Chapter-4	Performance Recognition	41
Chapter-5	Opportunity vs. Growth	46
Chapter-6	Power of Communication	53
Chapter-7	B +ve in Life	65
Chapter-8	Positive Attitude & Behaviour	69
Chapter-9	Leadership and Team Spirit for Quality	75

Chapter-10	Safety and Risk Assessment/Management	96
Chapter-11	Behaviour Based Safety Operations – a New Perspective Based on Transactional Analysis	106
Chapter-12	Beyond Politics to People	114
Chapter-13	Managing Stress	119
Chapter-14	The Rise & Fall of Human Power	137
Chapter-15	Institution Building: Individual vs. Social Responsibility	141
Chapter-16	Teacher vs. Mentor	148
Chapter-17	Thoughtful Thoughts	156

Part –II

Case Study	The Young Gun vs. The Old One By Prof. Nischal Mahajan	169
	The Author's Viewpoints on the above Case Study: Generation '(E) X' and Generation 'Y (oung)'	175

Epilogue 179

Foreword

In the last three decades there has been tremendous emphasis on Human Resource Management. Human capital assessment and measurement have become part of balance sheet in the area of business management and in every aspect where manpower is involved. The performance of human resources has become more complex with the advent of rapid technological changes where knowledge of workers is involved and even the thought process has been robotised. Basics of psychological aspects of team/group management and leadership qualities are more challenging now.

The prominence of Human resource management in brutally competitive world is universally recognised. The human resource personnel are now in top hierarchy with equal rank and power of their counterparts in technical and commercial functions.

Normally, books on Human Resources have been written mainly in three categories viz 1. With research based empirical findings, 2. Hard core text books for academic courses and 3. A blend of research findings, concepts and theories and their implications for practising managers. This book belongs to the third category.

Mr. R K Shankar is a practising manager in the field of Human resource management and total quality management. He is also a trainer and consultant in the field of Human Resources. His long experience of more than three decades in various organisations has inspired him to write this book so that valuable knowledge and practices are shared. He has largely covered all the aspects of human management and development. This book is written in simple and clear language avoiding complex technical jargons. This will make readers to understand the subject and use the knowledge to apply in their work environment. This will also be useful for the line managers in other functional areas. People are our greatest asset and therefore this book is about them.

New Delhi.
16th April 2018

Prof. (Dr.) R K Dwivedi

Preface to the New Edition

The **First** edition of this book – **"The Art of Managing Human Power"** was published and released exactly a year ago (May 2018) by **Notion Press. The book** has been made available online in their bookstore and through **flipkart, Amazon.in** & **infibeam**. The response to my book from the readers has been encouraging indeed and I take this opportunity to thank them for the same. From the numerous communication received by me from the students of business schools, fraternity of Human Resources and managers of many organisations, I am immensely pleased to know that the book has been found quite useful and has proved to be a simple guide for self and people management/development. As such, I feel, the very purpose of my writing this book is fulfilled to a great extent.

All along, the **First** edition has been available in India and in paperback edition only. In order to reach out to more readers across the globe and for their convenience, arrangements have been made with the publisher – **Notion Press** so that the revised and enlarged edition is made available now both in paperback as well as in e-book through **Kindle** worldwide.

I am sure, this would meet everyone's requirement and I am thankful to the publisher for giving wider options to our readers. The readers' feedback and suggestions are most welcome always as it enhances the scope for further improvement in the quality of this book.

New Delhi. **(R K Shankar)**
09th May 2019

Prologue

This book is the compilation of all my articles published in various journals & Newspaper with few additional chapters as well, so as to benefit my readers from the fraternity of Human Resources.

Broadly, there are four type of economic resources namely-**Land and natural resources** (soil, ore, oil, gold & other materials), **Labour** (Human Resources), **Capital** (man–made resources-machines) & **Entrepreneurship** (enterprise – which optimally utilises the above three in production and services). Among these resources, the Human Resources (Labour) and its functions are the most important as they are handling the other three resources including the enterprise. If any failure occurs in any of these 3 resources (Land, Capital & Entrepreneurship) the root-cause for such failure is the Human Resources and that is why they are called the **live-wire.** That is all the more reason the role of Human Resource Department assumes greater significance.

To start with, most of the organizations were either having an Administration Department or at the most a **Personnel Department** whose main function was to maintain leave records & disbursement of wages/salaries and labour welfare. When the organisations started realizing the importance of performance, productivity and competency more emphasis have been laid on Training & Development so as to ensure continual improvement in the performance & productivity of people. There has been a total paradigm shift in organizations' perspective – the amount spent on people towards training which was hitherto considered as an expense is now being viewed as an investment on Human Capital. That is how the emergence of Human Resource Department has taken place who acts as a link & fulcrum to all other activities in any business enterprise.

In fact if every individual in any organization starts acting as a human being (more empathetic –seeing from others' point of view & understanding their feelings) the role of Human Resource Department becomes simpler or may even be redundant. But unfortunately in a competitive world some people have become more self-centred & adopt all kinds of methods & means to rise in their lives at the expense of others. This is where the role of Human Resources' Head comes who is expected to act as a watch dog so as to protect the interest of the workforce in general & the organization in particular thereby ensuring their growth.

The sole objective of this book **'The Art of Managing Human Power'** is to develop every individual as a productive **Human Capital.**

Hopefully this would not only meet the requirement of Managers in any organization and students of business schools but also would help them to know themselves & others to enhance quality of life and the organizations, they are associated with.

Acknowledgements

This **'*magnum opus*'** has become possible only because of my long term association with the organisations where I have served over a period of 40 years in all.

The rich experience which I gained in the field of Human Resources from SAE (INDIA) LTD., which was subsequently taken over by RPG Group in 1995 with whom I served till April 2004 has enhanced my scope & career prospects especially in the area of Training & Development (T & D) and Quality Management System (QMS).

My present Organization **OCEANS XV Nautical Services Pvt. Ltd (who are basically involved in training the seafarers)** with whom I have been working as **Head (HR) & Lead Trainer and also as Management Representative (Quality Management System-QMS)** since its inception **(April 2008)** not only encourages me by giving new opportunities and challenges but also enables me to unearth my hidden talents. I express my sincere thanks to **the Directors of the company – Capt. Sanjiv Verma and Capt. Sanjeev Dhanda,** but for all their encouragements and able support my dream of this book would not have become true.

IMT (Institute of Management Technology), **Ghaziabad** had also recognised my contribution by publishing my article **'Leadership and Team spirit for Quality'** in their November 1997 edition of **"Sameeksha."** The improved version of the same is also reproduced in this book (please refer Chapter 9).

Further, by becoming **a Life member in National HRD Network,** I receive huge exposure which helps me to have continual improvement in the areas of my operation. Many of my articles were published in their **Newsletter** which I have compiled in this book.

The HR Journal **'THE HUMAN FACTOR'** – a then monthly publication of IIPM, New Delhi had published my viewpoint for a case study – **'The Young Gun Vs. The Old One' by Prof. Nischal Mahajan (Dean-Placements, IIPM-Hyderabad) in August 2009.** The same along with my viewpoint is reproduced in this book (please refer part II of this book) for readers' benefits.

Most importantly, I am indebted and grateful to **Prof. (Dr.) R K Dwivedi (the then President of erstwhile RPG Transmission Ltd. Between 1995 and 1998).** He was my mentor and guide during the period he was at RPG Transmission Ltd. where I was working then as Senior Executive (HR). It is a great honour for me to have his foreword for this book. In fact he and his book 'Organizational Culture and Performance (1995)' were the real inspirations for me in writing articles with the ultimate objective of coming out with this book which is the compilation of all my experience in the field of Human Resources.

Last but not the least, I place on record my sincere thanks to **'The Times of India'** who recognised my writing skill by publishing my maiden article **'Beyond Systems to people' way back in the year 1995 in their 'ÁSCENT' Bombay Edition (August 21, 1995).**

The improved version of the same article is reproduced in this book in the very first chapter as an overview of HRD for the benefit of HR fraternity.

I express my deep sense of gratitude to all the above organizations/ institutes and also to all my former & present colleagues who have been my source of inspiration to make this book a reality.

PART - I

Chapter-1

Beyond Systems to People – an Overview of HRD

Employees play a vital role in achieving the goals of the organization. Hence, it is imperative to have the optimum utilization of human resources to maximize the profits and achieve the targets of any organization. This is where the Human Resources Development (HRD) department comes into the picture. They identify the talents of the individual and his/her training needs to make an ordinary person an extraordinary one and highly motivated to fulfil organisational goal.

Manpower Planning

An organization can be successful only if it has adequate, capable experienced and trained personnel. It must recruit, select and place the right person in the right job. Management must plan the number and types of people which it wishes to recruit. This requires job analysis which calls for proper –

- Job design – assignment of tasks to jobs,
- Job descriptions – duties and responsibilities possessed by an individual; and
- Job specifications – qualification and experience required to perform a job.

Similarly five important factors are to be considered while making proper manpower planning, viz.,

- Forecasting futures needs of manpower.
- Developing a sound recruitment and selection procedure.

- Proper & effective utilization of manpower to foster the growth of the organisation as well as the individuals.

- Retaining the entrepreneurial and enterprising people through adequate compensation packages by giving them a sense of ownership and empowerment.

- Finally controlling and reviewing the cost of work involved through manpower.

Manpower planning avoids chances of overstaffing and understaffing. By anticipating manpower needs, organizations have the opportunity of developing existing manpower to fill the future gap through promotion. It gives encouragement to the existing employees and in turn creates a psychological climate for motivation. Manpower planning includes making employees development program effective, establishing industrial peace, reduction in labour cost through proper 'Human Resource Accounting Systems' and effective utilization of manpower etc.

Organisational Culture

Organisational culture refers to a system of shared meaning held by members that distinguishes the organisation from other organisations (Schein 1985). Organisational culture provides employees with a clear understanding of "the way things are done around here." Thus, a strong and healthy culture would be where organisation can have growth and active changefulness with innovativeness. This depends on leadership skill, trust, structure, reward, stress management, consideration, warmth, support and openness. A Healthy culture has an impact on the willingness of the employees to perform at their best.

Performance Appraisal System

In several organizations management have been deliberating on how to make an appraisal system more effective, goal oriented and performance linked. What could be the weight-age on different factors in performance evaluation? How the line, staff and service functions can be combined into one system? How transparent the system should be?

Loyalty Factor

Invariably, many instances can be seen in an organization where actual performance is ignored and final grading is done on the basis of a personal choice. More often than not the individual for whom one works is considered more important than the work itself. As a result, ultimate sufferers are those who are working not for an individual but for an organization. Thus the loyalty factor of an individual to the organization is not given due weight-age in the real sense. In the process, a new incumbent from another company is very often overrated and the employees who have put in long years of service in the existing company are underrated. Researches on the subject indicate that from the stand points of the superior and subordinates trust has been defined as the confident expectation of something involving the conditions of accessibility, availability, transparency, predictability and **loyalty.** If loyalty is ignored the employees with long service are de-motivated and their performances are adversely affected. The so called 'appraisal form' remains a mere piece of paper written and signed by the appraisee, appraiser, reporting officer, reviewing officer and performance review committee. To avoid this inherent problem, employees may be graded in the following manner:-

Grading of Employee

In an organization employees can be divided into three major categories namely,

- Excellent performer – who has entrepreneurial qualities and creative abilities, who welcome changes and consider them as opportunities and challenger rather than threats.

- Average performer – who just fulfils the tasks assigned to him.

- Poor performer – who fails to meet the targets within the given period.

One has to bear in mind that timely reward, creating greater scope for career advancement for excellent performers and recognition of their potential are very much essential so as to retain them and their talents and to make them extraordinary for the continuous growth of an organization.

As far as the average performers are concerned, the objective should be to make them good if not excellent performers. This can be made possible by the HRD department who can analyse and identify their training needs. By providing adequate & need based training their skills and knowledge can be upgraded thereby their competencies can be enhanced. Needless to mention here, they would ultimately become the real assets of the organization.

In order to handle the poor performers the HRD department can conduct counselling in the presence of their respective head of the department and the managing director/or the chairman of the Performance Review Committee (PRC) to understand their problems, give them the necessary advice, suggestions, reassurance to enable them to release their emotional problems and for their reorientation so that they can become average performers (if not good performers) over a period of time. One has to appreciate that counselling will not only rejuvenate a person but also help an organization in making suitable restructuring to adopt itself to the changes which are inevitable in and around the organization. In the event of not implementing the above steps, a complete de-motivation will emerge in the organization.

Many organizations nowadays adopt Bell-curve system of performance appraisal through which they try to segregate the best, mediocre and worst performers by dividing them in the following proportion:

1. High performers = Top 20%,
2. Average Performers = the middle 70% and
3. Poor performers = the bottom 10%.

The objective of this system is to nurture the best and discard the worst and to ensure normalization across functions, divisions and organization.

However, the Bell-curve model might turn out to be too rigid in cases where the employee strength in an organization is less. Here the concerned manager might be forced to place employees in specific ratings just for the sake of bell-curve requirements.

As per the bell-curve model guidelines, the managers can place only a limited number of employees in the top performers' category. In view of this rigid specification, some of the employees despite performing exceedingly well throughout the year might be forced to be kept in the Average performers' category just to meet the bell-curve requirements. This would lead to discontentment and loss of morale among those employees who marginally missed out the Top performers' category by a whisker. Therefore 360 degree feedback along with the bell-curve based normalization methodology would not only ensure a balancing act and well -rounded review but also would help in a more accurate assessment of the employees' performance .

Individual vs. Organization Targets

Here one has to appreciate that people have various needs and even the same person can have various needs at different times. Needs of an individual can be classified into two broader categories as per Maslow's theory of motivation as mentioned below:-

Lower Level Needs

Basic needs (food, clothes & shelter), safety and security needs (working condition, interpersonal relationship, job & social security for self & family). These are known as hygiene factors as per Herzberg theory of motivation.

Higher Level Needs

- Esteem and status needs –
    4. Recognition,
    5. Advancement in career and
    6. Ego and status.
- Self-actualization needs –
    1. Responsibility in work itself,
    2. Fulfilment and
    3. Achievement.

Thus, every individual has certain targets in his/her mind. To achieve his/her targets in life he/she involves himself/herself in fulfilling the organization targets. It is therefore needless to mention that once the individual's targets are met, an organization's targets can be automatically achieved.

Introduction of Self-Evaluation/Appraisal System

To enable each individual to assess his/her own performance many professionally managed and progressive organizations introduce Self Evaluation/Appraisal Systems which offers scope to each employee to mention his/her job description, (duties and responsibilities possessed by him/her) targets in the given period and his/her achievements in the same period. If any employee has any problem in filling in the form because of his inability to express vividly in English his/her head of the department should help him/her in filling in the same.

On achieving the targets specified by the person concerned within the stipulated period the head of the department has to give proper recognition by giving suitable rewards immediately. Thus the concept of time bound promotion based on qualification and experience may be replaced with promotion on achieving the stipulated targets. Thus the person who is receiving the promotion letter in appreciation of his/her performance and his/her head of the department who makes the recommendation to HRD department for his/her promotion will both have the equal satisfaction. Dissatisfaction and de-motivation can be reduced to the minimum if not avoided. Organizational goals can be easily met as more and more efforts will be put in by individuals in pursuit of achieving their own targets.

For any reason if the specified targets are not met by the individuals the reason for not achieving the targets have to be called for by the concerned head of the department either through personal interaction or through counselling as suggested earlier.

Exit Interview

In a well-developed organization the HRD department may call for an exit interview when an employee leaves them. The techniques may yield useful insights in spite of certain flaws such as:-

- Reasons for leaving are multiple.
- The employee may think that the chief reason would prejudice an employer if and when future references are desired/sought.
- Internal stress may make it impossible for a leaving employee to talk freely even to sympathetic listeners.

To avoid this, post-exit interview may be held after an employee leaves the organization and that too after he/she is placed in a secured job. Widespread discrepancies have been noticed by the organization in the reasons given by an employee in a first exit interview and post terminal interview. Following set of questions may be posed to avoid administrative flaws in future:

- Where are voluntary separations occurring?
- What categories of employees are leaving voluntarily?
- What early warning signals can be observed?

This will enable the organization to be cautious in future in retaining the employees.

Role of HRD

From the above, it is very clear that the involvement of the Human Resource Development department is so major that, it is engaged throughout the year in monitoring and achieving the organizational as well as the individual's goals. It thereby ensures that the organization does not suffer from any brain drain and thus goes well ahead in the present day competitive world especially with the advent of our government's liberalization policy.

Tour Report

Further, it is not out of place to mention here that people who are sent for out-station duties have to submit a report on their return mentioning in detail the purpose of their visit and the fulfilment of their tasks, along with an expense report which has to be reviewed by the head of the department. There should be scope for his comments in the tour report for improvement/suggestions for curtailing the cost and to make everyone accountable.

Chapter-2

Managing Human Power for Personal Effectiveness

Quality of an Organization can be assessed from the people engaged by them. Effective selection and retention of talent is feasible only when we have a strong Human Resources (HR) policies and proven practices. It is well known fact that all HR personnel have an excellent presentation skills as they act as an ambassador for the organization they serve by being customer centric. The HR Manager remains focused always as employees are their primary customers and their satisfaction assumes paramount importance for them. However mere lip service will not boost the morale of the employees and bring about the desired results unless, the HR Head practises what he preaches. Here let us analyse the role of HR in handling and resolving issues related to Human for **'Personal Effectiveness.'**

Setting objectives & Goals: For an Organization, the vision and Mission statement should be made clear to each and every individual directly or indirectly associated with the organization viz: employees, shareholders, customers & other stakeholders so that they work towards attaining the ultimate objective. Keeping the Organization's objective in mind, **the HR Head** while selecting candidates should have a clear foresight always and try to understand the minds of the new incumbents and their requirements/ambition vis-a-vis the organization's needs.

Action plan: The Organization can achieve its objectives only when proper planning is made and the blueprints are drawn. Action plan helps one to switch over from planning mode to execution mode. Each one of us expects timely delivery of products and services from our clients. However Quality of products and services are possible only if the required time is provided for production – which is known as the minimum gestation period; otherwise, it would be a premature delivery which will not give the customers the required delight which would be the ultimate aim. Further, availability of adequate infrastructure & logistics (viz: men, money, materials, time & space.) efficient and effective utilization of the same are to be ensured for increasing the productivity to stay ahead in the present day cut-throat competitive environment. For maintenance of consistency in product/service quality and timely delivery, we have to ensure not only assured performance but also speed of response by observing 'Time based Management' techniques where the importance of cycle time is given special emphasis. Reducing of 'Cycle Time' is possible only when we learn the art of distinguishing between important & urgent work and prioritize the same accordingly as shown in the following table:-

Table-I

Priority	Type of Work
1	Important & urgent from all sides
2	Not Important but urgent from the end user point of view
3	Important but not urgent
4	Not important and not urgent

One has to bear in mind that if timely pre-emptive action is not taken for important work it would become urgent. Similarly if urgent work is not attended timely it would be useless and would be a futile exercise even if it is attended later. Thus, one has to be discreet in understanding and evaluating the importance of any work so as not to invite any problem and to ensure consistency.

Consistency is the key: If one needs to be consistently a good performer throughout to establish his/her credibility, he/she has to control and discipline his/her activities. He/she has to set an example to others by his/her actions thereby, he/she can earn the confidence of his/her team members. It is possible only when he/she has the total commitment to the job assigned to him/her. Mistakes can be bare minimum if not avoided so long proper synchronization of body and mind takes place which can be made possible through **3D**s – **d**edication, **d**etermination and **d**evotion. After all, everything is based on mind over matter. However, it is a paradox that we learn more through failures than from success. All the same, commitment of repeated mistakes is the reflection of lack of concentration due to preoccupation of the mind with other problems/job presently not in hand which as far as possible needs to be avoided. Otherwise, it would be viewed as deliberate attempt to sabotage/short – circuit the system. By regulating our actions and observing the systems strictly without any aberration we can ensure consistency. This is possible only if we develop a positive attitude while dealing with a problem.

Positive Attitude: We have to bring in positive approach in resolving issues so as to avoid stress and strain. To feel great and remain positive always, one has to follow the principles:-

- Help others to the extent possible to help yourselves.

- Admission is always beneficial than hiding. Sooner we admit and realize our mistake is better for us otherwise we may have to regret later.

- Comparison with oneself rather than with others enables us not only to have introspection but also to adopt corrective and preventive measures to avert repetition of mistakes which ultimately leads one to continuous progress.

- Distinguish between physical and mental requirements – while the former to be met, the latter to be regulated if not controlled/resisted in the event of the former not accepting the latter.

Employees with a positive attitude will become a contributing member of the organization thereby, become an asset and indispensable. No wonder that Organizations are measured mainly by the attitudes of their employees. But, how to ensure their positive attitude even if they have to meet challenges consistently?

Changes and challenges: We must appreciate that in real life situation **only thing which remains constant is change.** Changes and metamorphosis are inevitable as the time goes by. People who refuse to accept the changes either blame others (aggressiveness) or blame themselves (submissiveness). In fact, the situations do not disturb them but the view of the situations that disturbs them. Unless we learn the art of adjusting ourselves to changes so as to bring about the required transformation within ourselves there is no scope for individual growth. In such an event, people need to be assertive and to consider changes as challenges rather than threats. Persons who upgrade their skills, knowledge & competencies (ability & desire to apply what is learned) from time to time through self-study & self-talk to keep abreast of the latest techniques will always have the tendency to accept the changing situations & will have greater scope for growth & success in life. If this cardinal aspect is understood well by the employees they can face any challenges boldly and would be a definite winner always.

In changing situations one has to give due importance to motivation which would act as an impetus to face any kind of challenges.

Motivation: Self-starters, self-beliefs, self-respect, self-confidence and self-motivation will go a long way in their future endeavours and bring in best results in oneself and the organization they serve. Any discussion on 'Motivation' would remain incomplete without making reference to Maslow's law of Motivation. Here we can view the same law in different perspective.

Table-II

Level	Quotient Type	Enables/Results in	With Reference to Maslow's Law of Motivation
1	Intelligent Quotient (IQ)	Logical conclusions viz: getting jobs, food & shelter.	To meet the basic needs, safety & security needs.
2	Emotional Quotient (EQ)	Inter/Intra personal relationship (viz: empathy & Emotional self-awareness), Stress Management (Stress tolerance & impulse Control) and adaptability – which ultimately result in optimism & general happiness.	Esteem & status needs viz: recognition, advancement in career position & power.
3	Spiritual Quotient (SQ)	Rational thinking results in fulfilment, achievements & responsibility in work itself.	Self-actualization.

Thus we can conclude from the above that one can attain self-actualization (the highest level of need) only when his/her 'Spiritual Quotient (SQ)' is high – a new concept in the theory of 'Motivation.' But when would a person reach this level is anybody's guess, as it varies from person to person depending on their value system and self-discipline.

However, to make the best use of different quotients viz: IQ, EQ & SQ at different levels in an organization, the HR Head has to adopt the proven "Performance Management System (PMS)" for getting the effective results.

Effective Performance Management System (PMS): The **PMS** is an important tool to enable Organizations to systematically plan, measure, monitor and review their business operations. By clearly establishing **Key Result Areas (KRAs)** for each employee the system ensures clarity, responsibilities and accountability for all employees and makes the process of assessment fair and objective. The PMS also reinforces the link between business results and pay and helps to recognize outstanding contributions made by individuals through **'Key Performance Indicators (KPI).'** It involves:-

- Performance Planning Process
- Performance Review & Assessment Process
- Development Planning Process
- Potential Assessment Process

The Performance Planning Process consists of the following two parts:-

1. Performance objectives-which should be **Specific, Measurable, Attainable, Relevant & Time bound.**

2. Performance competencies – whereby one's technical & business proficiency, innovation (out of box thinking), creativity (Development of the existing one or finding a new one), customer focus, team work & co-operation, setting & fulfilling commitments and communicating skills are assessed.

Through review & assessment process which includes self-assessment as well, the performance of the employees on their set – objectives and their performance competencies are rated by taking into account the **'critical incidents.'**

The objective of **'Development planning process'** is not only to enhance the competency level of individuals by upgrading their skills through training and development but also to measure its effectiveness for continual improvement.

Finally through Potential assessment employees' promotion/increments, areas of their strengths & weaknesses are decided. For Performance Evaluation, **S-M-A-R-T-E-R** (Viz: **S**pecific, **M**easurable, **A**ttainable/**A**chievable, **R**elevant/**R**ealistic, **T**ime-bound, **E**ffectiveness & **R**einforcement) rule is usually followed so as to have the **S-M-A-R-T-E-S-T** for the organization where **S** = **S**pecific, **M** = **M**easurable, **A** = **A**ttainable/**A**chievable, **R** = **R**elevant/**R**ealistic, **T** = **T**ime-bound, **E** = **E**ffective, **S** = **S**trategic & **T** = **T**eam. The final rating is done by taking into account the fact that neither performance nor potential alone can justify promotion cases. The following table will give you a true picture.

Table-III

Rating Scale	Traits	Remarks
4	High performer with high potential	Exceptional performer – Consistently exceeds expectations - an asset to the organization.
3	High performer with low potential	Achiever – consistency is maintained and sometimes exceeds expectations-a strong performer.
2	Low performer with low potential	Average – to be used only for repetitive and monotonous work as they cannot accept challenges and changes due to their limited potentials.
1	Low performer with high potential	Mere contributor as they are not reliable They try to live on past glories and would not take initiatives despite having high potential; they are liabilities to any organization and to be removed at the earliest opportunity as the organization would neither lose anything nor can afford such flab & frills.

One has to bear in mind that the ultimate objective of HR Head is not only to get the best people for the organization but also to retain them for ever so that they become the most sought after employer. However, the task of selection and retention process is very cumbersome for any HR Head.

Selection & retention: We must admit that nowadays selection and replacement cost have become very heavy. The organization has to adopt a suitable retention policy. The incumbents look for such organization which provide them decent pay & working environment, learning opportunities and career growth. The employer takes into account the following factors:-

- Opportunity cost-their market value
- Retention and development cost
- Replacement cost

An employer always ensures that replacement and development costs do not exceed retention cost by taking into account their intrinsic market value, age, experience and affordability. Whenever the retention cost is more than the replacement & development costs and the opportunity costs of the existing person is not as much as he/she imagines, it is better to go for replacement rather than increasing his/her salary or giving a promotion.

At the same time one has to remember that it is always worth allowing a person to go gracefully if he or she does not enjoy our work culture or if we cannot afford to meet his/her expectations or vice-versa. Every effort should be made to retain the relationship at least if we cannot retain the person by which we can get greater mileage. In the present scenario, the employers always prefer selective retention of those who score 3 or 4 in the rating scale as stipulated in Table-III, so as to hold the best at any cost rather than keeping all dead woods who cannot cope up with the challenges.

How much is too much? This is the most pertinent question and to be borne in mind always to get the best results. We must remember that even at times too much emphasis on any of the aspects mentioned in the above paragraphs will not bring about the desired results, as anything in excess is always bad. Even having too much of knowledge is of no use if it is not applied and shared with others. It is therefore essential to bring about moderation in every action to retain consistency.

The HR Manager plays a vital role in providing a balancing act in every situation. He/she acts as a coordinator between employees & employer thereby brings about a cohesiveness. While employees interests are considered and conveyed to the employer, he/she also makes sure that at no point of time the organizational interests are affected or compromised. No wonder, though he/she is the cornerstone of any organization he/she becomes the first casualty at times, if the systems are not in place or not strictly adhered to. It is therefore up to the organization and its people to use HR strategies to bring forth the best HR practices through Knowledge/Talent Management and Assessment/Development centers with special emphasis on working together and team work.

Chapter-3

Knowledge Process Management

Knowledge may be of two kinds – explicit and tacit. While explicit knowledge may be acquired through Data & Information, Tacit knowledge is possessed by individuals through insights and expertise which may not be visible to common man.

- Explicit knowledge which may be documented in manuals or stored in databases within the company; and

- Tacit knowledge which resides within people and represents skills, insights and judgments, technical expertise and practical know-how. It is acquired through personal experience, and is much more difficult to capture or document.

We in India by now, have realized that there is no dearth of potentials, resources of any kind & talents nor there are threats for 'brain drain.' In fact with the advent of globalization & liberalization policies and consequent inflow of Foreign Direct Investments (FDI), we have many gains which accentuate the faith reposed by foreign nations. Our country is being used presently as the backyard for Business Process Outsourcing (BPO) by the western countries and very soon would become the Knowledge Process Outsourcing (KPO) as well.

The Indian Diaspora in UK & US acts as ambassadors. They are a rich source of domain expertise who help transfer knowledge and expertise to India and nurture a new generation of India-based thought leaders. The living examples are Mr. Laxmi N Mittal with his audacious takeover of world second largest steelmaker Arcelor & Mr. Narayana Murthy by raising Infosys as one of the global IT majors through its inclusion in Nasdaq-100.

What we need to do at this juncture is to think globally and act locally. In other words, identify our strengths & weaknesses, provide opportunities to others to reveal their strengths, help them in overcoming their weaknesses or converting the weaknesses into strengths. Thus in an organization the HR Manager has to act as a mentor/coach by helping the line Managers and their team members to overcome their weaknesses & develop their strengths further rather than disdaining them. Even in the quest of fulfilling their Corporate Social Responsibility (CSR) this will help as it would ensure qualitative uplifting of people.

For effective application of knowledge, requires prevalence of wisdom which enables decision making process simpler and easier. Best decisions are made by people who understand the ground realities and make proper judgments of the situations. Apart from materialistic benefits, due weight-age is given for intrinsic value as well by prudent people. They achieve their goals by design and not by default. It may be remembered that merely acquiring knowledge is not adequate unless you learn how to effectively apply and share the same with others & that too at the most appropriate time so that you achieve your desired, distant and distinct results in life.

Ideally speaking, whoever converts his/her hobby into profession becomes successful in life ultimately because s/he knows s/he is best at what and also understands her/his strengths and weakness better than anybody else. In fact, the best would come off a person only when s/he enjoys what s/he does. For obvious reasons, his/her performance would be at its peak when s/he is doing her/his hobby. Developing a hobby into profession is easier as s/he has the natural instinct/craving for the same.

This is what the HR Manager in an organization has to look at in a person. By identifying his/her natural talents/potentials at the time of recruitment, the HR Manager has to facilitate him/her in developing his/her natural talents by giving enough opportunities through

Development centre so that s/he may derive the maximum pleasure from his/her job and simultaneously the organization would also reap the rich benefits through him/her. Neither dissatisfaction/frustration nor exploitation would be experienced by anyone in the organization and the best quality of life is also ensured by this process.

Shall we give a try if not done so far?

To be fair, there is nothing right or wrong in this world. What is actually needed in a Society/Organization is a regulatory mechanism which should be strictly observed by all concerned, just like playing a game as per the rules. One has to understand the rules clearly and has to pay the penalty if s/he breaks the rules. The norms are to be framed taking all factors into considerations without any prejudice to anyone.

For example, wearing of **'burqa'** by women in Saudi Arabia is mandatory and has to be strictly adhered to. Similarly if one is not wearing helmets while driving scooters on Delhi roads the police would take cognizance of the same and impose fine immediately.

So, please remember 'Do in Rome as Romans do' to have a trouble-free life.

Chapter-4

Performance Recognition

Organization's development can be made possible through consistent performance from its employees and continual process improvement. To ensure both which are essential to have a competitive edge in the global economy, more creative and innovative ideas need to be encouraged across the board. Thus for both consistent performance and continual process improvement it is imperative to keep the morale of the employees at the highest level by focusing on the essential motivating factors.

Recognition & Motivation: All of us expect others to acknowledge our views, recognize our work & initiative and appreciate our actions. A word of appreciation acknowledging our good deeds will do us a world of good and motivate us to look beyond our designated areas. However, neither Performance nor potential alone can justify Promotion. Similarly, neither Promotion nor Increments can be used as a tool for Motivation. In fact, Promotion is a tool for recognition and reward for work & competencies whereas, Increment is a tool for reward for work done in the immediate past. Both Promotion & Increment add to the feeling of well-being of employees.

Support & Expectations: First of all we should be clear whether 'Employee Development' Program is designed primarily for immediate benefit or to meet the long term goals of the Individual and/or the Organization? We must have realized by now no individual can grow without getting the support from his/her organization. At the same time no individual can get the support unless he/she has the potential and commitment to deliver results. Thus, whenever a person supports another it means that he/she has identified the other person's potentials and therefore has high expectations from him/her. This is applicable in every walk of life.

Expectation of a coach/mentor from his team members, expectations of parents from their children, expectations of an organization from the employees are examples to mention a few.

If the team members perform well, the coach/mentor get elated otherwise he feels disappointed and so is the case as far as parents or organizations are concerned with respect to their children/employees. Thus, both Support and Expectations go together. This can be delineated through the following Table.

Table I

	(ii) High Expectations & Low Support	(i) High Expectations & High Support
	(iii) Low Expectations & Low Support	(iv) Low Expectations & High Support

↑ Expectation

→ Support →

The 1st quadrant of the Table reflects High Expectations & High support from the Organization/Mentor/Parents which is a very healthy sign for growth. Work will be fun for employees, team members & children which will act as a motivating factor for them to consider changes as challenges. Ambition, aspiration for growth, development & achievement will always be there amongst them as they will have a sense of belongingness & self-beliefs.

The 2nd Quadrant depicts exactly the opposite. Since the expectations are high & support extended is almost nil by the Organization/Mentor/Parents the stress level among the employees/ team members/children is very high as they feel they are totally burnt out, experience insecurity & helplessness and sometimes even feel that they are being exploited. They look for an outlet and at the earliest opportunity want to quit/leave the place for better environment as they feel suffocated. Leave aside the ego clashes, the employees/team members/children lose their self-respect even which is very unhealthy and in the process one may lose even the best people which is disastrous to the industry/family.

In the 3rd Quadrant, since both expectations & support level are at the lowest level there will be apathy, boredom all over with a feeling that nothing gets done. The future will appear to be bleak as the work will become dull & monotonous.

Contrary to this in the 4th Quadrant one will get maximum support from their Organization/Mentor/Parents though their expectations from their employees, team members & children will be very little. Everyone will be in their comfort zone and will remain complacent as well. They may be pampered always which is not an ideal situation in the long run though the present atmosphere may appear to be quite conducive. This is due to the fact that they are not exposed to the external pressure as they have never been stretched nor their potentials have been tested. They have no vision & mission in life and therefore their future would become darker. Unless they plan for future through proper preparation, perseverance, prioritizing, regular practice and of course, with sustained patience without succumbing to pressure by displaying commitment, competency and confidence consistently they cannot ensure brighter prospects.

From the above we can understand that the ideally 1st quadrant would be the most desirable and preferred one for continual improvement.

Johari Window Model: While discussing on the importance and implications of Support/Expectations for continual process improvement it is worth remembering one's strengths & weaknesses and understanding the concept developed by Joseph Luft & Harry Ingham at the University of California in the year 1955 popularly known as **Johari Window Model.** It is represented in the form of a window with four Quadrants, as depicted below.

Table II

(A) Known to self & others	(B) Not Known to self but known to others
(C) Known to self but not Known to others	(D) Not known to self & Not known to Others

Quadrant A reflects all the strengths and weaknesses known to self as well as to others which may be called as an **Open area (Arena).** In this Quadrant one's strengths & weaknesses is known & accepted by the other in the team.

Quadrant B covers such strengths and weaknesses that self is not aware of, but others happen to notice the same and therefore may be known to be **Blind spot.** So long others appreciate his/her strengths & weaknesses and know how to make best use of him/her there is absolutely no problem. But the moment they start ridiculing one's weaknesses instead of helping him/her in coming out of the weaknesses or converting the weaknesses into strengths the trouble starts. Thus the role of a coach/mentor/organization is to help the team members to overcome the weaknesses and develop their strengths further rather than disdaining them. In other words, they should act more as a facilitator than as a dictator to get the best out of their team members.

Quadrant C includes such strengths & weaknesses that self is aware of, but not disclosed to others which is known as **concealed or closed area.** Here the self is concealing certain facts which he/she may be though aware that what he/she is doing is not correct. Son not smoking in front of parents is an ideal example for this. Similarly, boss not offering seat to his subordinates during discussion is though considered as a disgrace but their displeasure never communicated to their boss which is not good for either of them as there will always be some kind of undercurrent between them.

Quadrant D refers to such area which is known as **Dark area** where neither of them is aware of their strengths & weaknesses. In such condition one has to do some self-discovery so as to assess their respective strengths and weaknesses and help each other in overcoming their weaknesses and enhancing their strengths.

Thus we can conclude from the above model that wider we make our **Quadrant 'A' the more successful we become.** In other words our policies and practices should be open and transparent without having any hidden agenda to lead and build our team for future.

Chapter-5

Opportunity vs. Growth

"Life must be understood backward. But it must be lived forward."

— **Soren Kierkegaard**

"If we would sell our experiences for what they cost us, we would all be millionaires."

— **Abigail Van Buren**

"All of us do not have equal talent, but all of us should have an equal opportunity to develop our talents."

— **John F Kennedy**

All the above quotations emphasize the importance of experience, talents and opportunities for success and growth in life. There is a saying that everything is fair in love and war which is being abused and misused in the present day competitive business world by adopting all sorts of ambush marketing to grab opportunities & power. Ideally speaking, one has to be fair to oneself & others to enjoy *win-win* situation rather than *win-lose or lose-win scenario* so as to have mutual benefits.

In fact, no one knows more than you what is best for you as you only know your real strengths and weaknesses. Hence before availing any opportunities, one has to do S-W-O-T Analysis *viz:* analysing one's **S**trengths, **W**eaknesses, **O**pportunities & **T**hreats. We have to ask ourselves why a person looks for opportunities? – either he is aspiring for growth as he finds no scope in the present environment or he is not enjoying the present environment for various reasons or may be both. In either case, especially when he/she is not getting the timely and due recognition in the present set-up, he/she has to explore the external opportunities to prove a point to others and to know his/her real worth. In the event of getting an offer, the next question he/she has to ask himself/herself whether he/she has the requisite competencies and potentials to excel well in the new job/offer which he/she has received.

Sometimes it is quite possible, the organization making the offer are desperately in need of a person so as to handle their present crisis without having any long term goals either for its organization or for the new incumbent. In such a situation, the person who gets an offer though may feel initially that he/she has got a breakthrough but may realize soon that it was only a temporary gain, once he/she was dumped there too, after the prospective organization's short term goals are met. Thus the concerned person would soon land up in the same position if not worse than where he/she was before joining the new organization. It is acceptable though to look for better opportunities, but while choosing the alternative, one has to be discreet otherwise they would put themselves into greater and deeper troubles.

Thus, whenever a person gets an offer however lucrative it may be, it is prudent on his/her part to get more details about the organization from where he/she received the offer. Further he/she has to ascertain whether the position which is offered, is an existing one or a new one created in view of their expansion/diversification plans. If it is an existing one, it means he is being recruited as a replacement and in such an event under what circumstances the earlier person is leaving or forced to leave, have to be understood clearly. This would clarify where the fault lies-on the person concerned or on the part of the organization? In the event of the former you may be careful while taking over the job from him/her and in the latter case you may review your decision again about joining the organization as it raises doubts about its track records. A frank discussion about the offer (though not necessary to disclose the name of the organisation) with your immediate boss in detail before putting down the paper will also do a world of good. This would not only give your boss sufficient time and scope to ponder over the issue but also enable him/her to give his/her views.

After all, he also knows your strengths & weaknesses because of your long association and would reassess the matter by trying to find the actual reasons which had prompted you to look for an alternative. He would also try to be fair to you as well as to the organization while handling your resignation. In case, he felt the organization would be the loser if you leave and also reconciled to the fact that timely and due recognition since not been given to you which led you to look for better opportunities elsewhere he would make his best efforts to convince you and the decision making authorities in the organization (The CEO, the Managing Director and the HR Head) with the intention of retaining you. All along the organization/your boss would have misunderstood your loyalty factor and taken you granted for ever and would have never anticipated any threat from you. Having realized their mistakes, they would try to retain you by making fresh offers and assurances. You may reconsider their fresh offer with an open mind, as the known devil is always better than the unknown monster. One has to bear in mind – our aim is to enjoy the work & the environment and not to leave anyone in lurch. Thus quitting the present job should always be the last resort.

If your present boss and organization show indications that they had been enjoying your work all along and try to understand your feelings and make suitable amends in their treatment towards you by making fresh offers to please you as well, you may always stay with them once there is a scope for getting rejuvenated is assured. On the other hand, if the organization and your boss do not show any signs of shock once you put down the papers then you have to understand that this is what they were expecting from you and had you made any further delay in finding an alternative, they would have shown you the door which would have turned out to be a greater disgrace to you and your self-respect.

From Organization's Perspective: Attrition whether drive-attrition caused by the employer's policies or drag-attrition because of employees ill-feeling has become a threat for the organization in general and for the HR Division in particular in retaining the employees in spite of making the best offers to the incumbents while selecting the persons. To reduce attrition and ensure retention of best people, the organization has to evolve proper policies and practices and let the same be known to the incumbents at the time of selection either through campus interviews or otherwise by making proper presentation so as to avoid any ambiguities later. The most professional Companies like Tata Consultancy Services Ltd. (TCS LTD.) always make their **Vision (Global Top10), Mission** (To help customers achieve their business objectives) **& Values** (Leading Change, Integrity, Respect for Individual, Excellence, Learning and Sharing) public so as to give and earn confidence from all its stakeholders.

Most of the organizations do not present the true picture about their organizations and sometimes try to show a rosy picture to their incumbents without even having a blue print. No sooner the incumbents come to know the realities they start looking for elsewhere.

Providing employees' hand book, offering Career Development Plans, giving career counselling and planning career paths to its employees help to control attrition. While recruiting employees the HR Head has to take into consideration the opportunity cost, replacement cost and retention cost so as to strike a balance between them and to ensure a blend of youth and experience which is desirable for an emerging organization. The rule of horses for courses to be adopted and therefore merit should be the sole criterion and caste, creed & sex should not come in the way of promotion whether it is public sector or a private enterprise so as to throw challenges to all.

The Performance Management System (PMS) should be suitably designed to translate Vision and Strategies into objectives and actions. It should be the guiding tool for the entire organization to stay focused and create department level targets. The Organizational goals and individual's role in achieving the goals should be made clear to each individual by the HR Division through the line Managers. The individual goals are developed based on department's targets so that each employee has objectives/goals/KRA (Key Result Areas) that are measurable and are aligned to the organizational goals which would ultimately help in achieving the same in a concerted manner. The entire thing depicted below in the form of a diagram.

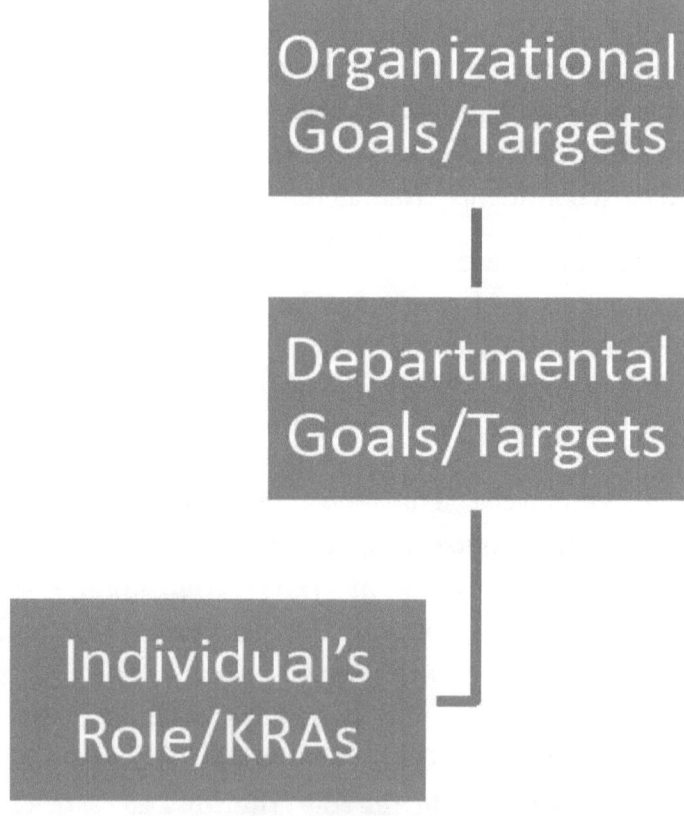

Fig. 1

Opportunity vs. Growth ▪ 51

Individual's view point: Everyone is career conscious & ambitious in life and always in search of opportunities and growth. But sometimes they are disappointed as they fail to draw a line however fine it may be between what they desire and what they deserve. At times they also suffer from insecurities & threats within and outside the organization because of the prevailing stiff competition which make them to look for other opportunities.

All of us face such issues daily, though some are within our control while others are not as they are beyond our control viz: rising prices, natural calamities like tsunami etc. But the time and energy spent/lost/wasted on issues beyond our control are disproportionately higher and are really alarming as shown in the following diagram.

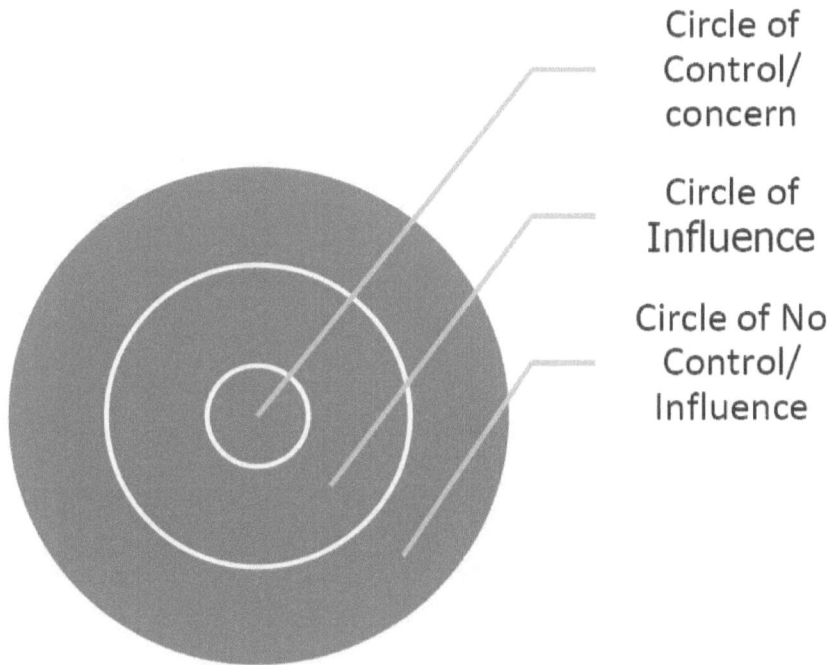

Fig. 2

There is no point in wasting our energy and time on which we have no control which would exude only negative thoughts. Instead one has to be proactive and put in efforts to make things happening so as to get the best results for him/her as well as for the organization where he/she is attached to.

So, what can help an organization/its employees to achieve their targets/goals and who can be the enabler?

The answer to the first question is to have a two-way communication at all levels to avoid any ambiguities and to encourage transparency. The enabler of course is the HR Manager who should act as a facilitator rather than a dictator by providing all guiding principles and practices to the line Managers. He plays a significant role in transferring the knowledge of people Management to the line Managers. Thus, Collaborative approach would be the key to an effective partnership which ultimately leads an organization to success.

Chapter-6

Power of Communication

Communication is one of the most important functions of management to bring the people closer and work together for achieving organizational goals and objectives. It is widely acknowledged now that the success of any business to a large extent depends on the efficient and effective communication. Lack of proper communication is the root cause for many organizational failure and therefore due importance needs to be given for the same.

What Is Communication?

The term **'Communication'** is derived from the Latin word **'Communis'** which means **common.** Thus **Communication** involves rendering common ideas, opinions or information that is, sharing of ideas, opinions or information. According to Keith Davis, "Communication is the process of passing information and understanding from one person to another." It is a way of reaching others with facts, ideas, thoughts and values.

Characteristics of Communication

Based on the above definition, following are the basic characteristics of communication:-

- Communication involves at least two persons – the sender and the receiver.
- To be effective, it should always be two and not a one way process. Therefore, feedback from the receiver to the sender

is an essential component of communication without which it becomes incomplete.

- It is a dynamic process in the sense that it grows and develops.

The flow of communication is depicted below in fig.1.

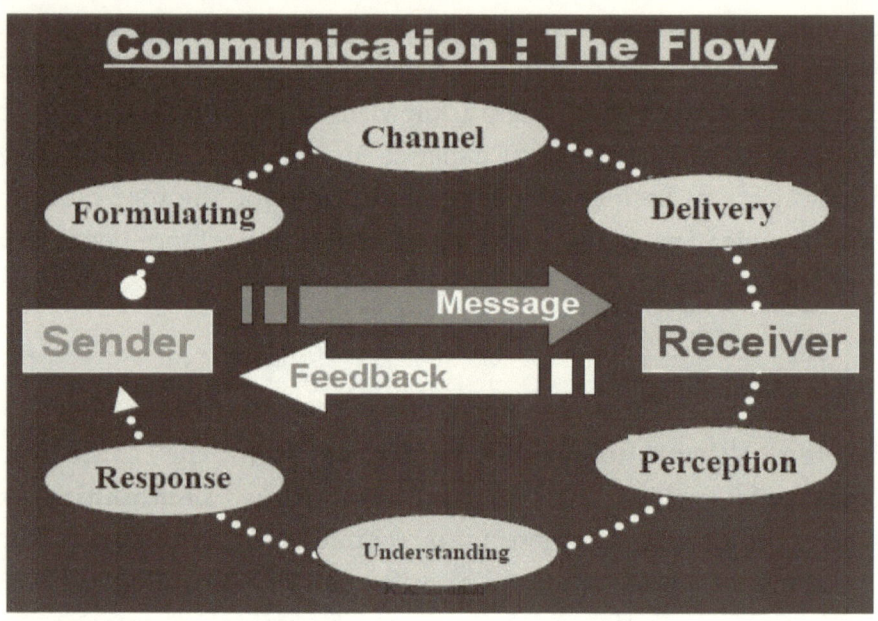

Fig. 1

Classification of Communication

Communication in an organization can be broadly classified into two types:

- Formal
- Informal

This classification is based on channels of communication. The channels of communication refer to the path through which the information is transmitted.

Formal communication refers to the official communication which follows the formal channels established by the organization. It can be oral or written. Oral communication can take the form of interviews, meetings, presentations and so on. Written communication can take the form of notes, memos, letters, reports etc.

Informal Communication on the other hand refers to communication between individuals and groups which does not follow the official recognized channel. In other words, it is a social interaction among the various members of the organization. The transfer of information may be related to work or other matters and it cuts across official lines of communication.

Both types (formal and informal) have their own merits and limitations. Information obtained through formal communication though may be more reliable and accurate, its scope for flexibility is very minimal as it is less responsive. Whereas, through informal communication we may get more information as they are more flexible and responsive; however it may lead to grapevine & rumours which is not good for any healthy organization in the long run. Ideally, we have to maintain a balance between the two by having one to one communication/discussion at regular intervals to overcome the deficiencies of a formal mass communication.

This deficiency is known as "Abilene Paradox" which can be understood from the following story:

On a birthday, a family decided to go out for dinner. Husband asked wife, where to go?

Thinking that he likes Gujarati food, she said: "Let's go to Agashiye – The Terrace Restaurant!"

His son and daughter nodded in agreement.

On their return, the son remarked, "I wish Papa had taken us to Mainland China, as he loves Chinese food."

"Or at least to Shere-E-Punjab for the wonderful tandoori chicken," added his daughter.

"Yes, I too would have loved to go Mainland China!" the man said.

Wife looked surprised: "But didn't we all unanimously agree to go to Agashiye?" she asked.

He said sheepishly "I didn't want you to feel bad." And both children nodded in agreement.

Here were four people who of their own volition would not have gone to Agashiye – The Terrace Restaurant, but collectively agreed to go there.

This could have been easily avoided had there been an informal communication on one to one basis.

This also happens in the Corporate World. This is the Abilene Paradox.

Prof. Jerry Harvey calls it 'The Inability to Manage Agreement.'

The Abilene Paradox occurs when a group of people collectively decide on a course of action that is contrary to the preferences of most of the individuals in the group.

Prof. Harvey states in his paper 'The Abilene Paradox,' "Organizations frequently take actions in contradiction to what they really want to do and therefore defeat the very purpose they are trying to achieve."

He adds, "The inability to manage agreement, not the inability to manage conflict, is the essential symptom that defines organizations caught in the web of the Abilene Paradox."

In the corporate world, when the top boss throws an idea, the group immediately agrees. This is because everyone in the group thinks he would look stupid if he disagrees. Standing out as a lone voice is very embarrassing. This leads the group to decide on 'yes' when 'no' would have been the personal (and the correct) response of the majority. If the top boss always disagrees with rest of group, then the organization will never have group giving honest opinion.

From the above, we can conclude that when the communication becomes too formal, effective and decisive results cannot be achieved.

Importance and Essentials of Communication

The importance of one-to one communication should be appreciated, otherwise it may lead to delay, dilution and distortion of information which would adversely affect the decision making process to a great extent and in turn would result in chaos and confusion. It is therefore essential to acknowledge, repeat and give the feedback in one-to-one communication so that there is no ambiguity between what is said/heard/conveyed which will ensure clarity and remove all confusion and doubts.

Example: On board the ship, when a crew was asked to pay out the port anchor the crew heard as both anchors and paid out both inadvertently.

In another instance, when the duty engineer asked one of the motormen to close valve no. 1 to 5, the concerned motorman closed only valve no. 1, 2 and 5 instead of closing all the 5 valves.

In both the cases, the confusion could have been avoided if the persons receiving the instruction had acknowledged, repeated & given the necessary feedback. We must remember, the pronunciation varies from person to person based from different countries.

Further, we have to follow the **KISS principles – (keep it short And simple)** – in communication to get the desired results. Apart from that timing of communication also matters to a great extent – wrong communication at the right time and right communication at the wrong time would prove to be disastrous.

In addition to the above, the following **'7 Cs'** need to be observed for effective Communication:-

1. **Clear:-** When writing or speaking to someone, be clear about your message and its purpose. If you are not sure, you cannot expect the receiver to be clear either. To make things clear, try to minimize the number of ideas in each sentence. You should not expect the receiver to read between the lines and make assumptions/presumptions on his/her own.

2. **Concise:-** When you are concise in your communicating statement, you stick to the point and are brief as well. Write down what you want to say point by point in a sequential order and delete the inessentials.

3. **Concrete:-** When the message is concrete, the receiver gets a clear picture of what you are trying to convey. If there are details and vivid facts, the message would acquire the required importance.

4. **Correct:-** When the communication is accurate and error-free supported by facts and figures, needless to say that it would appeal and attract the audience/receiver.

5. **Coherent:-** When all points are well connected, relevant to the main topic, logical and the flow of text is consistent then it is considered to be coherent.

6. **Complete:-** When the audience/receiver gets everything he/she needs for taking the necessary follow-up action, then the message is complete in all respects.

7. **Courteous:-** Courteous communication is friendly, open and honest. They are cordial and explicit giving due respect to the receiver.

Another important aspect in communication is **'listening.'** Ability to listen is much more important than ability to communicate. **"When you talk, you are only repeating what you already know. But when you listen, you may learn something new." – Dalai Lama.** Half of the problem can be easily resolved if we give a patient hearing to others and therefore maximum weight-age is given for **'Listening (45%)'** among the means of communication which is shown in the following fig. 2.

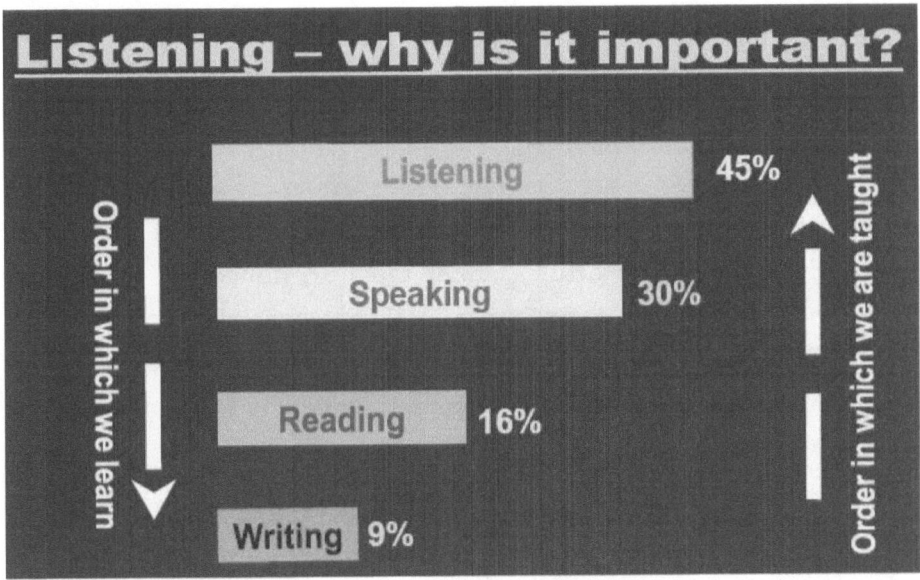

Fig. 2

From the above (Fig. 2), the value of listening can be understood easily. But unfortunately, our education system is such that emphasis is laid more on the written answers to questions. That is why, Human Resources Department gives equal weight-age for interviews, viva etc. while selecting the persons for any position as they give scope for assessing their attitude and behaviour apart from evaluating their skills and knowledge.

The art of listening can be observed by the following methods:-

- By asking more questions-both open ended (in the form of what, how and why) and close ended (who, where and when) questions, we can get all our doubts cleared.

- Reflect our feelings by showing empathy (see from others' point of view also).

- Convey reassuring message through our body language (non-verbal cues, viz: nodding, acknowledging and smiling at the appropriate time etc). All these will give a clear indication that we are listening intently.

- Avoid anger which is one letter short of Danger and we should never get provoked easily as we would be the loser. Even when the other person talks all nonsense, we should not be argumentative or critical, however right we may be. Other person's own statement can be used against him at the most appropriate time especially, when it is related to any investigation matter.

- Remember, the main purpose of asking questions/cross examination is to get as much facts/inputs/information as possible for making appropriate decision.

It has to be appreciated that communication is an on-going process in any organization and in order to be effective we have to remain focussed on the following fundamentals as well:-

1. **Think before communicate:-** Many communications fail because of inadequate planning. If we fail to plan, it means we are planning to fail. Good planning must consider goals and attitudes of those who will receive the communication and those who will be affected by it on receiving.

2. **Know our objectives:-** Before any communication, we should be clear about the purpose and objective of what we want to accomplish. It is meant to obtain information/initiate action/gain understanding of new policy or procedure/change another person's attitude/refute charges by union officials/dispel fear caused by false rumours. Having said that, it would be unwise to try to achieve too much with one single communication.

3. **Know the audience:-** While communicating, it is essential to take into account the experience, attitudes, feelings and expectations of individuals/group we are dealing with. The physical and human setting of the audience at the receiving end will largely influence the impact of a communication.

4. **Consult:-** It is desirable to consult others (involved directly or indirectly) in planning a communication. Such an approach would provide additional insight and objectivity to the message. The main advantage of such consultation would be that those who have been taken into confidence while planning through communication, would extend their support during implementation phase as they would be made to feel as part of the team. Needless to mention, team work would provide the necessary synergic benefits.

5. **Determine the Medium:-** After having decided the subject matter, it should be determined as to how best this message has to be communicated. All aspects of oral and written communication including usage of multimedia viz: Television, Newspaper, Magazines, Social media (whatsApps, tweets etc. to name a few), internets, emails etc. have to be carefully examined. In case of necessity the communication has to be in bi-lingual (English and local language) especially if it is addressed to all levels of the organization.

6. **Filtering of information:-** Too much of information is as bad as too little information. We must therefore refrain from loading irrelevant information. Before we communicate anything to anyone we need to ask ourselves three things: 1. Is it true?, 2. Is it essential to share? & 3. Is it harmful by sharing? – In other words, authenticity, accuracy and validity need to be verified so as to exercise control over flow of information.

7. **Support with action:-** It is highly necessary that we must practise what we preach which would have a huge impact. This is because action speaks louder than words. It should be noted, the most persuasive communication is not what one says but what one does.

8. **Climate of trust and confidence:-** While communicating with people in our organization, we have to build a congenial environment to win their confidence and trust. Subordinates need to be convinced that the organization is truthful and sincere in its intent.

9. **Check the results:-** It is not superfluous to mention here that the purpose of communication is not complete with mere transmission of message. It should be ascertained whether the same was received in the manner intended and the response was appropriate. The receiver should be encouraged to express his/her reaction in the form of **'feedback'** to evaluate whether the communication has been understood and acted upon or any adjustments/modifications are needed.

10. **Use gender-neutral language:-** While addressing the staff/employees use words like **workforce/human-power** instead of the word **"manpower."** Similarly, Chairman of a company may be addressed as **"Chairperson."**

Some of the ways in which an organization can improve its communication skills can be summarised as under:

1. Don't oversell an idea.
2. Don't give up efforts in communication too soon. Persistence pays off in the long run.
3. Timing is very important. Choose an auspicious moment to make the announcement.
4. Plan your communication carefully before it is circulated.
5. Keep it short & simple and to the point.
6. Anticipate objections and have well-prepared answers ready.
7. Invite participation from all persons/groups.
8. Provide adequate time for discussion before making decision.
9. Give all participants the feeling that they have not only been heard but also their apprehensions/doubts have been cleared.
10. Learn to say and hear **'NO'** wherever necessary. We must appreciate, saying **'NO'** and not doing is better than saying **'Yes'** and not doing as it amounts to making false assurances/promises.
11. **The 3 Rights** – 'Right to know,' 'Right to refuse' and 'Right to participate' need to be effectively used to derive the best results through communication.
12. Establish an impression that final decision has been arrived at by consensus.

Thus, the main idea of communication is to keep everyone in the loop which is vital to the rejuvenation of all organizations. The potential for micro-communicating needs to be explored as our organizations and society have become more connected but less in touch physically and emotionally. Training supervisors and managers to communicate effectively must be the top priority for any organization aiming for continual improvement and growth.

Chapter-7

B +ve in Life

Life as a whole consists of so much uncertainties that we expect guarantee & warranty on everything to ensure safety and security. We must remember however that nothing in this world is permanent and the only thing which remains constant is **Change.** We must upgrade our skills & knowledge and make some value addition daily so as to have continuous growth and success in life. All the same, we all know that without taking risks, we cannot grow in life. Greater the risks are higher the scope for either fall or windfall. Risk Analysis, Risk Assessment and Risk Management are imperative to take adequate precautions for our well-being. The basic question here is how to manage risks and to approach a problem with a positive frame of mind during period of crisis? Let us read further to get an answer and to remain *+ve forever.*

Opportunities keep knocking at our door always. It is up to us how we make the best use of available opportunities especially, when we have no choice and the opportunity available has scope to meet our ultimate objective without making any compromise in our value system. However when we have more than one option at our disposal the right choice can be made after evaluating the pros and cons of the various options. It all depends on our perceptions – our mental approach in an environment based on past experience.

We should never reject an existing offer in anticipation of a better offer in future as we know, *one bird in hand is worth more than two in the bush.* Later on when we actually get a better offer we can find ways to come out of the present arrangement by explaining our position & without straining the existing relationship. In fact, situations in this world do not disturb us but it is our view about the same which disturbs us. An example will elucidate the point more clearly.

The CEO of a multinational shoe manufacturing company wanted to explore the company's market potential in an African country and sent his Marketing Executive there to make an assessment. The Marketing Executive came back within a week's time and submitted his report to CEO stating that it would not be possible for them to market their shoes in that country as no one was wearing shoes there. Since not satisfied with the report and the reasons given by him, the CEO sent another person to make a feasibility study. The second person on his return reported that there was excellent scope for marketing their shoes in that country as no one was wearing the shoes there. He suggested in his report that if they could convince the people over there the advantages of wearing shoes by adopting suitable marketing strategy they could capture a huge market there for their shoes.

The observations of both the persons were though uniform there had been huge difference in their inference as the former's view was totally negative and the latter's was absolutely positive. It is needless to mention here that the company could achieve amazing results based on the suggestions given by the latter.

We can give innumerable examples like this to emphasize the importance of positive approach in handling problems and finding solutions for continuous growth. Few years ago using cellular phones and having computers at homes were all considered luxurious. Nowadays even an auto driver and a house maid carry a Mobile phone to provide prompt and better customer service. These are signs of positive changes in our everyday life.

To err is a human: In our everyday life and even in our profession we make mistakes. Sooner we realize the same is better for us to take corrective and preventive actions thereby reducing the damage to the bare minimum. If we have the tendency to hide mistakes or shift the blame to others, the factual position would come to surface soon and we have to pay a heavy price for the same.

Remembering the help received from others rather than talking about our good deeds would do a world of good to us always as the former reflects our intentions to return and the latter reveals our expectations from others. The moment we start expecting from others, our good deeds lose its sanctity. Similarly brooding over the past mistakes is a sheer waste of time which would not help anybody as it would only act as an impediment in our thought process and hinder our progress. In this context we must remind ourselves the following always:-

- **Past** has become history which can be used as a reference for future actions.
- **Future** is always a mystery and therefore it should not worry us much.
- **Present** is a gift for us in our life always and that is why it is called present.

Thus we should learn to live our present life fully to reap its rich benefits. Thinking of problem itself is a problem and similarly the fear of failures will lead to more failures and all of us should realize these fundamental rudiments in **Life**. In short, **Life** has to be either enjoyed or experienced and there is no other third way to live. From each experience we learn a lesson or two which in turn provides maturity of thoughts. Once our Thoughts get matured we derive pleasures and clarity in Life. We must bear in mind that problems in our **Life** are to be addressed and not to be advertised if we have any desire to progress.

Similarly, Students while pursuing a course should be clear about their career beforehand. One should not do any course just for the sake of doing. He/she should be aware of his/her strengths and weaknesses and accordingly should choose a course to make a successful career.

If one cannot decide on his/her own he/she can seek the help of counsellors and well-wishers (parents, teachers, relatives and friends) before joining a course. He/she should never aspire to choose a career just because it is quite popular, lucrative and commands respect in the society viz: Medicine, Engineering & MBAs etc., if he/she does not have the right aptitude to do so. The thumb rule is that one should do what he/she feels that he/she deserves rather than what he/she desires. One should never adopt any short cut methods in achieving his/her objectives just because he/she wishes. It must be borne in mind always that any short cut methods would lead to short circuits causing huge damage to us. The willingness, ability, capability and affordability are to be given due considerations while choosing the objectives otherwise, one has to pay a heavy price later. Further, accumulation of qualifications and knowledge has no relevance if no proper application is made by them in real life situations. A person with a positive mind develops interest on subjects he/she likes most by listening and questioning. Further, he needs concentration, patience and intelligence to analyse its intricacies to remain focused.

Evaluation of one's strengths and weaknesses is a must and capitalization of the strengths rather than thinking about the weaknesses would do a world of good to individuals. A successful Manager is one who has the ability to understand what his team members are best at and make use of their knowledge and skills in the best possible manner to achieve the organization's objectives.

The positive psychology helps people to make things happening rather than watching things or wondering about how it happened.

Why don't we start applying now before it becomes too late?

Chapter-8

Positive Attitude & Behaviour

Attitude is an evaluative statement or judgment of an individual concerning objects, people or events. They reflect how one feels about something. Attitudes lead people to behave in a fairly consistent way towards others. We need to have a positive attitude and should not get affected by situation, objects and people (SOP) to enjoy peace, security and happiness forever which is the sole objective of our life. Many times our behaviour pattern is based on our emotional attachment/ detachment or past experience and the same is reflected in our attitude towards others which need not necessarily be correct. We might have had a bitter experience in the past with someone, but we should learn from our mistakes and make sure that the same is not repeated again and move on instead of complaining about the same. In other words, we should approach a problem with an open mind and not with a preconceived notion.

We all know, different people have different needs and the same person has different needs at different times also as the priority changes over the period of time. At the age of 5, the children would be happy with chocolates and ice-creams; when they grow and become 15 years old, they may be tempted to watch some adult movies secretly in their parents' absence; when they become 25 years old they would love to own a car after getting well employed; and needless to mention, when they turn out 30 years they would like to have a home and family of their own to lead a comfortable life.

The above fact has to be kept in mind by an organization while engaging people. Once this aspect has been taken care of well by an organization by giving the required facilities and timely recognition for their employees' contributions in the form of promotion, they may observe a very positive attitude of their employees towards their job and responsibilities which would contribute about 85% for the success of the organization; whereas, we will be surprised to know that the aptitude (skills and knowledge) of individuals contribute only 15% towards the success of an organization. It is more like an iceberg phenomenon where only 15% is visible to us and the remaining 85% is below the sea level. The visible part may be correlated with our skills & knowledge and the invisible part of iceberg which is below the sea level is like our attitude which is more important. Obviously, we can therefore claim that the attitudes and not the aptitudes of employees determine the altitude and growth of an organization.

No wonder, the HR professionals at the time of selecting any person for any position always try to give emphasis more on the attitude of new incumbents than on their aptitude; it may be noted, without required qualifications and experience generally nobody applies for any job as it is the minimum prerequisite. Verification of qualification certificates is a mere administrative matter and therefore the HR professionals focus more on assessing their attitudes while interviewing candidates. Some candidates in order to impress the interviewer, may say that emoluments are not their main criteria as they are more interested in joining such esteemed organization to have more exposure and experience. But when the interviewer makes an offer of $3000 for the job, the candidate may immediately react by saying that $4000 are being offered by other companies for the similar jobs and thereby they get exposed as their statements may turn out to be contradictory to their earlier claim. The Inconsistency in their statements would expose their attitudes and thereby they lose the opportunity of joining the company despite having an exemplary qualification certificates.

We must remember, the value system which we follow should match with the value system of the organization with whom we are attached; the standard set by an organization needs to be met; our judgments need to be clear; business ethics need to be followed and we need to have the self-belief as well – which are the real reflection of our attitude and will have a definite impact on our behaviour pattern. A positive attitude is not the destination but needs to be our way of life. It is not extraneous to say that our positive thought is the real seed for the positive results.

Whether the glass is half full or half empty depends on the attitude of the person looking at it. Needless to mention here, the person with a positive way of looking at things would say that the glass is half full. However, HR professionals would be more realistic in their statement by saying that the glass is too big for its contents. They always talk in terms of right-sizing so as to remain fair.

We must therefore remember that a pessimist complains about the wind always; an optimist expects and waits for it to change and the realist adjusts the sails or alters the course according to the situation.

In this regard, a small inspirational story is given below with the view to change our attitude.

One day a professor entered the class room and asked his students to prepare for a surprise test. The students waited anxiously at their desks for the test to begin. The professor handed out the question paper with the text facing down as usual. He asked his students to turn the page and begin. To everyone's surprise, there were no questions – just a black dot at the centre of the page.

The professor seeing the expression of the students told them the following,

"I want you to write what you see there!"

The confused students got started on the inexplicable task.

At the end of the class, the professor took all their answer sheets and started reading each one of them aloud in front of all the students.

All of them without any exceptions, described the black dot, trying to explain its position in the middle of the sheet, etc. After all had been read, the professor began to explain:

"I am not going to give any grade on this to anyone. I just want to say something to you to think about. None of you wrote about the white part of the paper. Everyone focused only on the black dot – and the same happens in our life. We have a white paper to observe and enjoy, but unfortunately we always focus on the dark spots. Our life is a gift given by God to us with love and care and we have always reasons to celebrate-nature renewing itself every day, the friends around us, the job that provides our livelihood and the miracles we see every day. However we insist on focusing only on the dark spots – the health issues that bother us, the lack of money, the complicated relationship with a family member, the disappointment with a friend etc.

The dark spots are very small compared to everything we have in our lives, but they are the ones that pollute our minds.

Take your eyes away from the black spots in your life. Enjoy each one of your blessings and each moment that life gives you."

So, the most significant change in a person's life is the change of attitude. Right attitudes produce right actions and it all depends on us whether to remain happy or not. We must remember, the pessimist sees the difficulty in every opportunity; whereas, the optimist sees opportunity in every difficulty. The positive thinker sees the invisible, feels the intangible and achieves the impossible. The man who has confidence in himself gains the confidence of others as well. One can go as far as he/she thinks he/she can go. We therefore should not run away from the problems or avoid situations where we might make mistakes. Courage is not the absence of fear but overcoming the same to face any kind of situations. Our life is a reflection of our attitudes. Positive attitudes create a chain reaction of our positive thoughts. We must remember always, no one fails if he/she puts in his/her best efforts though the results sometimes get delayed but not denied.

According to Henry Ford, "If you think you can, or you think you can't, you are right..."

So, if our thinking process becomes positive our attitude and behaviour pattern also become positive. The first and foremost thing is that we have to bring in change in ourselves by way of a positive thinking. But unfortunately instead of changing ourselves we try to change others because we do not want to come out of our comfort zone which is not at all good for us. Well, the only person who welcomes the changes is a baby with the wet diapers. We must admit that the diapers are mainly used for the convenience of the mothers albeit causing discomforts to the babies. If babies can talk from the day they are born they may ask for the change of diapers very often or may raise their hands against diapers as they cause lots of discomfort to them.

An organization can initiate steps for changing behaviour of their employees to make them think positively. When their employees' are unconsciously incompetent and are not aware that they don't know they resist any change as their potentials are low and so are their performance level. In order to make them aware of their deficiencies, the organization has to provide them the required training and exposure. On getting such exposure, the concerned employees understand their incompetencies and develop willingness to perform better despite having low potentials. However the organization can develop their abilities also apart from their willingness by imparting more training to them. So when their skills and will are developed further their performance level would also improve drastically; it is quite possible, the concerned employees may be unconsciously competent-which means, they don't know that they know. At this stage, the company would be in a position to extract the maximum work from such employees to increase productivity as their potentials and performance level must have enhanced considerably. However, the company should not exploit their potentials as there is a huge difference between extraction & exploitation.

While extracting maximum work from employees, the organization not only helps them improving their strengths but also enables them to overcome their weaknesses. On the other hand, exploitation means the company points out only employees' deficiencies and weak areas but no words of praise/compliments given for their positive contributions that will obviously demotivate them which in turn will bring down their performance levels slowly. So if the organization expects a consistent performance from its employees they should send them for repeated training to upgrade them as and when there is a change in technology. Needless to mention here that when employees are consistently trained and developed their morale become high; however, we should also ensure that they don't become overconfident when their potentials and performance both go up simultaneously. Because overconfidence is as bad as the lack of confidence and this is where the HR Manager plays his/her vital role to keep everything and everyone in check and balance so that his/her attitude remains positive always and effectiveness of the training is ensured.

Well, when the attitude remains positive the organization can enjoy a good team work which is essential to have the synergic benefits. **TEAM** means **T**ogether **E**mpowering each other to **A**chieve **M**ore/**M**aximum/**M**iracles or we can say, **T**otal **E**ngagement of **A**ll **M**embers... So, unity in diversity is possible only if we have the right attitude towards everyone/everything.

Chapter-9

Leadership and Team Spirit for Quality

Human Resources Management (HRM) has assumed greater significance in recent times in achieving organizational goals through identifying the training needs and imparting the same to individuals thereby enhancing their competencies by upgrading skills and knowledge on regular basis for continual improvement of the Human Resources. One will appreciate that optimum utilization of Human Resources to maximize the profits and reach the targets of an organization can be made possible only by the Chief Human Resources Officer (CHRO) who acts as the coordinator/facilitator for the entire organization.

By giving timely rewards to great performers, the organization can not only succeed in retaining them and their talents but also can ensure that their morale is kept high always for effective results. But we must also be conscious of the fact that all performers cannot be made as leaders, albeit all leaders are expected to be great performers consistently. Here comes the role of **leadership** into the picture. The **leadership** has to take the following steps/initiative to build a dynamic team:

- **Drive people:-** Map out your team's mission statement, define its purpose of existence, chart out the team's goals and priorities & make the "rules of the road."

- **Strive hard:-** Clarify team members' roles and responsibilities, set realistic goals, identify roadblocks and draw up action plan.

- **Thrive:-** Provide feedback, commit to conflict resolution, collaborate for creativity and deal with decision making – Empowerment.

- **Arrive:-** Celebrate success, keep track of progress, consistently encourage involvement and revitalize team meetings.

- **Revive:-** Unwelcome intrusions/change plans/restructuring of department, need to backtrack few steps to regroup, re-establish team's goals, priorities and re-look at responsibilities.

One will appreciate, as the time changes the technology also changes and therefore one needs to be on the learning course always throughout his/her career.

Let us discuss at length about the qualities of leaders and their styles of functioning to develop excellent team work in an organization, in the absence of which synergic benefits can hardly be had which is very much essential for successfully attaining the organizational goals.

In short, we can say, **Team efforts -> Individual efforts + Group efforts.**

Definition of Leadership

According to Keith Davis, "Leadership is the ability to persuade others to seek the defined objectives enthusiastically. It is the human factor which binds the group together and motivates it towards its goals."

George R. Terry defines leadership as "Relationships in which one person (leader) influences others to work together willingly for which the leader desires."

Real leaders are those who develop more leaders rather than followers albeit without followers there can be no leaders.

Leadership Is the Key to Success

A leader has to lead by example and has to lead from the front; he has to be selfless and should be a source of inspiration to his followers by his action. Then only he would be able to earn respect rather than command respect. One has to bear in mind that respect cannot be demanded but has to be earned, by setting goals, providing a sense of direction and making subordinates work for results. A leader has to stimulate actions by giving orders to subordinates and by supervising them through two-way communication (which involves feedback as well) and effective motivation as they proceed with their work. The subordinates always prefer a boss to be someone who they respect and admire not because he is on a higher managerial level, but because he has the potential to lead them by virtue of his knowledge and experience & who brings about cohesiveness of individuals' efforts towards accomplishment of enterprise's objectives. He must be prepared to sacrifice for his people/organization and should be a role model. In short, people always prefer to be led rather than just managed by their boss. Because according to Peter Docker, "Management is about handling complexity and leadership is about creating simplicity."

Frontline Leadership

In most of the business organizations today, there is no dearth of human resources though they suffer from lack of managerial capabilities at the top level. They fail to perform the basic functions of management viz. planning, organizing, directing, co-ordinating and controlling which are obviously essential for achieving the objectives of an organization. Management is basically getting things done by and through people. The authority delegated to a leader/supervisor must be prudently exercised in relation to people so as to get the desired results from his subordinates. According to Simon Sinek, "The responsibility of leadership is not to come up with all the ideas… but to create an environment in which great ideas can thrive." Thus by giving empowerment to his subordinates, a sense of ownership and belongingness can be created amongst them so that innovative ideas may emerge.

Adoption of TQM & TBM Techniques by Leaders

The modern Total Quality Management (TQM) techniques emphasize 'Right things at the right in the first time' to enhance productivity and quality of products produced and services rendered so as to maximize the stakeholders' satisfaction. Quality Management basically involves – Quality planning, Quality manual, Quality control & Quality improvement.

The need of the hour is to develop a 'Quality philosophy' in the organization and a systematic approach to Quality Management so that, products produced and services rendered add values for the customers and thereby provide them not only satisfaction but also give them the required delight, which is the ultimate **"benchmark."** One will appreciate every product that is sold and every service that is rendered always acts as an ambassador because every customer who receives the same gives the necessary advertisement for the product/service.

Here we must know the meaning of 'Quality.' In simple terms, Dr. Juran defined Quality as 'Fitness for use.' We divide quality into **"Product Quality"** and **"Service Quality."**

Product Quality is decided by customer's needs, conforming to specifications, assured performance & safety, proper packaging, timely delivery, efficient technical service and incorporating customer's feedback.

In case of Service Quality, speed of response, dependability, control and facilities become important factors.

ISO (International Organization for Standardization) defines quality as "Totality of features and characteristics of a product or a service that bear on its ability to satisfy stated or implied needs."

Quality Management System (QMS) is based on PDCA (Plan-> Do-> Check-> Act) cycle to ensure continual improvement and the same is briefly described below:-

PLAN:- Establish the objective and processes to deliver results in accordance with customer requirements and organization's policies (What to Do? – objective and How to Do it? – Procedure).

DO:- Implement the process – Do what was planned.

CHECK:- Measure & monitor the processes and the product against policies, objectives and requirements & report the results to check whether things have happened according to plan.

ACT:- Take actions to continually improve process performance (How to improve next time through corrective actions).

We can understand the same clearly from the following figure given in the simplest form:-

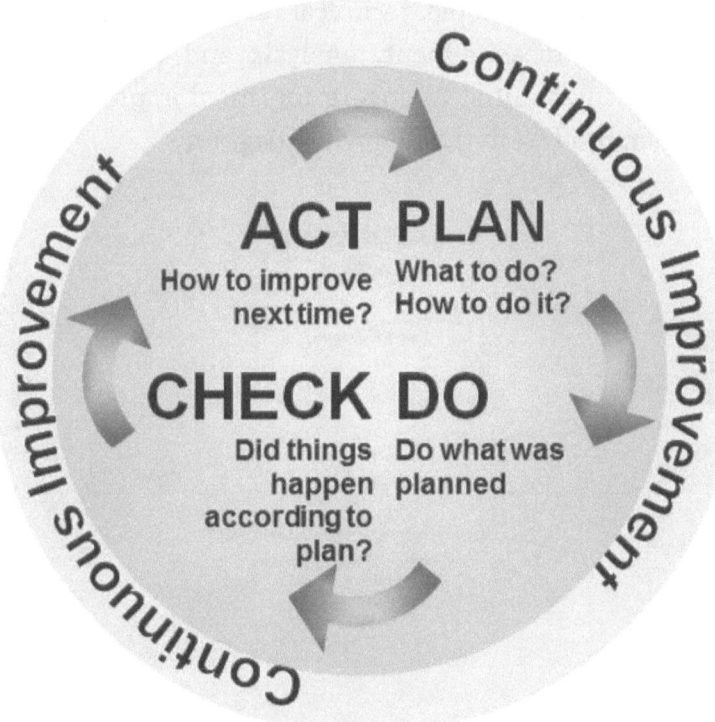

Fig. 1

It may be noted that the PDCA Cycle is a framework for executing **Kaizen** technique to ensure continual improvement. **Kaizen** is a Japanese word where **Kai** means *'change'* and **Zen** means *'for better.'*

So, Change for better can be made possible, if we divide the job into small tasks and attempt to make improvement in every task on a continual basis.

For continual improvement, we need to focus more on the effectiveness than on the efficiency because we are concerned more with the results than with the efforts. Effectiveness is realised when planned results are achieved whereas efficiency is the mere use of resources and efforts. For effective results/output of the Quality Management System (QMS), we need to draw a process mapping for every activity which involves inputs, methods/procedures, risks/opportunities, control, people, technical resources and other support services. Further, measurement, analysis and monitoring of the processes are also essential to ensure continual improvement. It can be easily understood from the following diagram:-

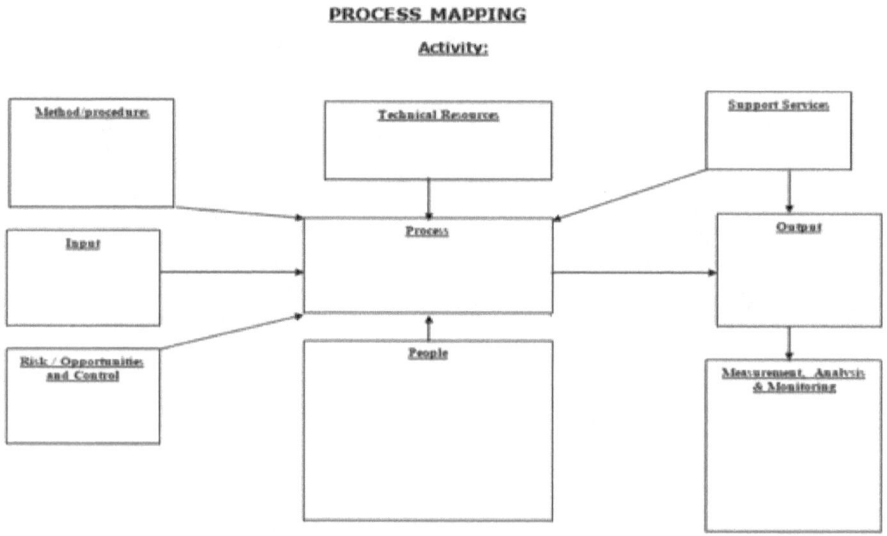

Fig. 2

In this regard, we must remember the following:-

- All activities are (part of) a process.
- Every process has one or more objectives.
- Each process has steps.
- Each process has inputs & output and
- For each process one or more performance indicators are identified to ensure continual improvement.

The ISO 9001:2015 version calls for risk based thinking so that preventive actions are envisaged beforehand for all operations by remaining proactive always rather than reactive. Further, more emphasis on leadership and authorities/responsibilities of top management have also be defined well for organizational development on continual basis.

While assessing the risks and opportunities involved in any process, we have to understand and analyze both internal and external environment in the context of the organization. The Organization shall monitor and review information about these internal and external issues to understand how they will influence the quality system on a continual basis so as to ensure that it meets the strategic planning, vision, mission, quality-policy and business objectives.

Internal Environment: We need to draw a proper organization structure so that hierarchy and position are defined well and there are no ambiguities or overlapping of responsibilities and authorities. Further, we have to identify functions that need to be outsourced so as to ensure there is no dearth of resources. Understanding the internal context can be facilitated by considering issues related to organizational values, culture, knowledge and performance.

External Environment: Similarly, understanding the external context can be facilitated considering issues arising from legal, technological, competitive market, cultural, social and economic environment whether international, national, regional or local.

Needless to mention here that the ultimate objective of the quality management system is to protect the interests of all stakeholders-customers, owners (shareholders), employees, bankers, regulators, suppliers, partners or society that can include competitors or opposing groups.

Now, the TQM Techniques is slowly getting replaced with a radical new efficiency technique – Time Based Management (TBM) which is expected to leave the competitors far behind. The future war-cry will therefore be "Survival of the fittest."

The TBM theory is fairly very simple. It believes that cycle time is the most critical parameter of efficiency simply because everything else is linked to time. A modern leader who gives importance to training, re-training and business process re-engineering can succeed in reducing the cycle time by optimum utilization of men, money, materials, time and space. Thus by taking less time to accomplish any given task, we will be able to achieve higher level of productivity.

There are many models that can help the organizations to understand the strategic nature of their industry and how they fit into that environment. The simplest model that can be used is **S-W-O-T** analysis where **S = S**trengths, **W = W**eaknesses, **O = O**pportunities and **T = T**hreats.

The organizations have to improve their strengths, overcome their weaknesses and should have the ability to distinguish between opportunities and threats so that decision making process would become simpler and easier which would enable them to be the ultimate winner.

Classification and Styles of Leadership

The various types of leadership have been classified by several management authorities in different ways. The Path-Goal Leadership theory was formulated originally by researchers at the University of Michigan. It was developed by Martin Evans and Robert House independently. The distinct feature of this theory is that it recognizes the positive relationship between leadership and motivation.

The Path-Goal theory attempts to explain the impact that the leader – behaviour has on subordinates' motivation, satisfaction and performance.

The types or styles of leadership according to House are:

1. **Autocratic/Directive Leadership:** This type of leader initiates rewards and penalties. His subordinates feel inferior to him and are generally passive. Their morale is not high and there is no scope for developing future leaders among them, though they know exactly what is expected of them as specific directions are given by such leader. Thus an autocratic leader is one who commands and expects compliance without any participation in the decision making process by the subordinates.

2. **Supportive Leadership:** Here the leader initiates actions for others, has a high frustration-tolerance and is sensitive to the feelings of others. He gets the job done but does not develop a leader, albeit the leader shows human concerns for his subordinates.

3. **Participative Leadership:** This kind of leader helps others to develop their own initiative, to take their own decisions & formulate their own procedures and allows them to recognize their own wants thereby wins their co-operation for achieving his objectives.

4. **Democratic/Achievement Oriented Leadership:** This leader sets challenging goals for subordinates and reposes confidence in them to attain the goals. Here, mutual trust is a must for achieving results.

One can find from the above that the type/style 1 and 2 leaders are more autocratic in nature with style 1 very severe & style 2 relatively considerate. On the other hand, type/style 3 leader is very much consultative in nature. He allows his subordinates to participate in decisions but reserves the ultimate right to make decisions. But you can observe that type/style 4 is an absolute democrat allowing total participation and deciding on the basis of consensus.

The aforesaid 4 styles of leadership can either be effective or ineffective depending upon the extent to which it is used as shown in the figures given below:-

Effective

S1-> Directing	S2-> Problem Solving
S3-> Developing	S4-> Delegating

Fig. 3

Ineffective

S1-> Dominating	S2-> Over involving
S3-> Over accommodating	S4-> Abdicating

Fig. 3 (a)

Where S1-> Autocratic Leadership style,
   S2-> Supportive Leadership style,
   S3-> Participative Leadership style,
   S4-> Democratic/Achievement Oriented Leadership style.

Suitability of Leadership Style

Autocratic style will be effective during emergencies when the time is short and the leader has to lead from the front giving directions/orders. He needs to be assertive but not aggressive to have effective results. When he is assertive he gives reasons why it should be done/why should not be done. Whereas, when he becomes aggressive he gives orders without giving any reasons as he feels he is not answerable to his subordinates; this is more like dictating or dominating his people and in the long run he will not succeed in retaining the best people with him as nobody would enjoy working under such leader because s/he gets demoralized by such dominating style.

Supportive style can be adopted when people have to do some monotonous/frustrating jobs, voluminous/stressful work, repetitive and laborious work where more hands are required and not much brain needed (psychomotor operations). Here the physical strain may lead to mental strain also and therefore the leader has to give his subordinates the required time/space/breaks and tools so that they don't become physically and mentally tired; he should go to his people as and when he finds time & allow his people to have an easy access with him to resolve issues. He should not be in a silo so as to derive the best and effective results through them. But this style would become ineffective when he visits/disturbs his people too often to know the progress of the work as it would irritate them and in turn would prove to be counterproductive. To have the best results under this style, the leader needs to have regular periodical review-meetings /briefings with his subordinates to assess the progress of the work and to equip them with the necessary inputs for necessary corrective measures wherever needed to ensure timely completion/delivery.

Participative style will be useful when a leader (CEO) has to deal with different departmental people in the same levels. While handling peers he has to ensure that no ego clashes come in the way of achieving the organizational goals. We will appreciate, one-upmanship feeling may impede progress of the work and therefore the leader has to be conscious of the fact that nobody is suffering from inferiority/superiority complex. He has to develop them by identifying their training needs and imparting the same to them so that they acquire the required level of competencies for discharging their tasks/duties and responsibilities. He has to share information and obtain inputs from them so that everyone is kept in the loop. But we have to keep in mind here that the subordinates undergo such need based training that the scope for immediate application is possibly made available so that the organization enjoys the fruits without any loss/waste of time, money and energy. Otherwise, there is every danger of losing such people to other organizations/competitors through poaching who lure them with better offers or by promising them with better prospects/opportunities. In other words, it would turn out to be as though we train people for other organizations which would prove to be detrimental to the interests of the organization.

Democratic style will be the best suited when ambiguous, non-repetitive and innovative tasks have to be performed where more ideas have to flow in. By delegating powers, the leader may create a sense of belongingness in the minds of subordinates which would inspire them to come out with more innovative ideas for organizational growth/benefits. However, he must monitor the progress to ensure that there is no aberration in the direction provided to them. Here it should be noted, the leader should not abdicate his responsibilities; otherwise, the subordinates may feel insecure/not protected and have been let down by his leader. If subordinates make any mistakes, the leader should resolve the issues quickly so that no major damage occurs; similarly, if anyone makes some invaluable contribution on the projects on hand, it should be recognized/complimented and to be brought to the notice of others so that he gets motivated. In other words, criticism should not made in public but compliments to be made in front of others which would do a world of good for the entire team in achieving the targets.

One must bear in mind in this context that energy by itself is neither constructive nor destructive. It is up to the individuals as to how the energy is utilized – either for productive purposes or for non-productive purposes. Similarly, any kind of leadership style can be made effective or ineffective depending upon the extent to which it is adopted.

According to Rensis Likert, there are 3 variables that affect the relationship between Leadership and Performance in an organization which are enumerated below:-

1. **Causal variables:** Organization structure, Management policies and decision, Leadership style, skills and behaviours are considered causal variables.

2. **Intervening variables:** These represent the internal climate of an organization. These variables have a say on or affect inter-personal relationships, communication and decision making in an organization. Performance goals, attitudes, loyalties, perceptions, motivation etc. are important intervening variables.

3. **End-result variables:** These are dependent variables leading to outcome in an organization. They are productivity, costs, service, profits etc.

As per Likert, there is no direct cause-effect relationship between a causal variable and an end-result variable. For example, there is no direct relationship between leadership style and profits. But intervening variables viz. attitudes, loyalties, motivation etc. play an important role in bringing about changes in the end-result. Because of this process (the effect of the intervening variables) there is considerable 'time-lag' in the end-result.

For instance, if style-1 leader (autocratic/directive) is appointed at the start of the business he might get good performance-results immediately, but at the same time his style of leadership would have an adverse effect/impact on the intervening variables viz. loyalties, attitudes, motivation etc. Assuming that because of his good results, the style-1 leader is promoted and a style-4 leader (democratic) takes over his place. However, due to the effect of the 'time lag' the intervening variables viz. motivation, loyalties, attitudes etc. affected adversely by the previous leader (style-1) will come into effect now. As a result, the performance under style-4 leader (democratic) might decline. Hence the style-1 leader (autocratic) might replace style-4 leader (democratic) to enhance performance of the organization. At this time, the intervening variables activated by the style-4 leader will start bearing fruits and the company's performance starts increasing and the credit may again go to the style-1 leader though he does not deserve in the real sense. This cycle will be on for the years to come and the style-4 leader's contribution may go unnoticed forever.

Thus, Rensis Likert had established that managements are often guilty of wrong evaluation/conclusion as they fail to take note of the positive effects of intervening variables while making assessment.

Therefore the management while assessing any type of leader in an organization should not only give due weight-age to the effect of such intervening variables but also consider the impact of 'time-lag' on the end-result variables to make a fair performance evaluation.

We must remember a good leader inspires others with confidence in him; a great leader inspires them with confidence in themselves. Hence while building the team we have to assess the will & skill of the people to extract the best out of them.

1. If the subordinates have **the low will and low skill,** the leader has to give/show them guidance/direction.
2. If they have **the high will and low skill,** the leader has to coach/train them.

3. If they have the **high skill but low will,** then the leader has to motivate/support them.

4. In case the subordinates have **the high skill as well the high will,** their leader has to delegate the powers to have the desired results.

The same is depicted in the chart given below for easy understanding (refer Fig. 4).

In nutshell, we may say, we need to adopt the right kind of leadership style according to situations. In other words, situation-based leadership style will provide the effective results for any business enterprise.

However every leadership style has its own limitation and may lead to certain conflicts and the same is delineated in the following pages.

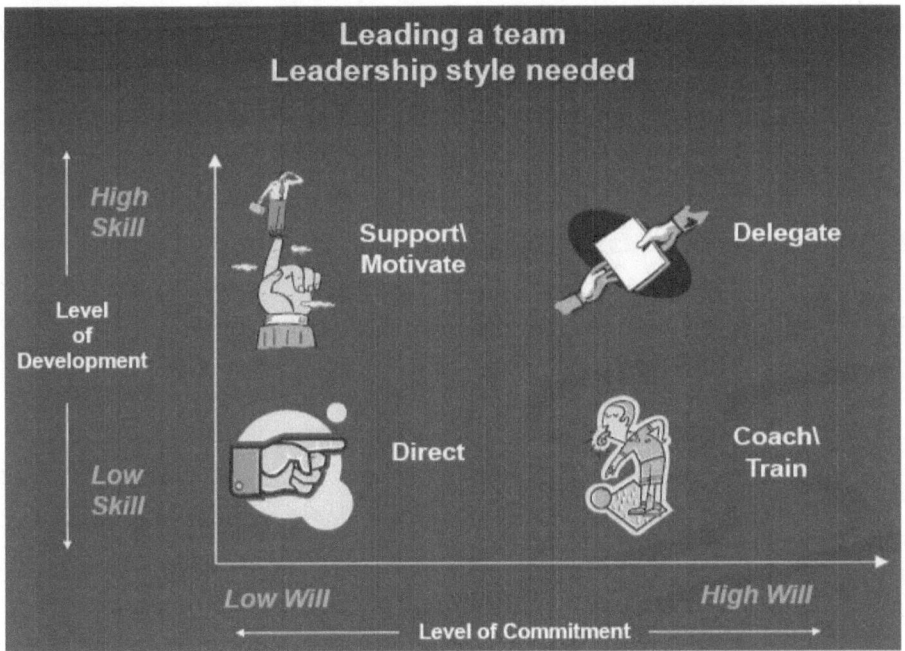

Fig. 4

Conflict Management

The condition in which the concerns of different team members appear incompatible is known as conflict. Conflict is inevitable given the wide range of goals for the different stakeholders in the organization.

The Thomas-Kilman Instrument (TKI) model assesses the individual's behaviour in conflict situations. We can describe a person's behaviour along two basic dimensions – a) **Assertiveness** towards tasks-the extent to which an individual attempts to satisfy his/her own concerns, and b) **Co-operativeness** towards people – the extent to which he/she tries to meet other person's concerns. These two dimensions of behaviour can be used to define five methods of dealing with conflict. These five conflict-handling modes are given below (Refer Fig. 5).

1. **Avoiding (1.1):** This kind of leader is neither assertive nor cooperative. When an individual joins an organization and if he/she is neither getting the required co-operation from other people nor given the guidance as to what he/she has to focus at, he/she will lose interest in the organization sooner and would try to leave the organization at the earliest opportunity especially when he/she senses that there is no scope for survival in the organization. The absence of co-operation acts as a de-motivating factor for him/her to stay in the organization as the conflicts may surface from the day one itself.

2. **Competing (1.9):** This type of leader is assertive, uncooperative & in a power-oriented mode. When competing, he/she pursues his/her own concerns at other person's expense, using whatever power seems appropriate to win his/her position. Competing might mean standing up for your rights, defending your position you believe is correct & simply trying to win at any cost by being ruthless. Here the leader of an organization may be more focused towards organizational goals but would be hardly concerned about new

incumbent's problems. This kind of leader would be however effective only during emergencies and would be a total failure in other circumstances. Even during emergencies also, the leader has to adopt assertive style and not aggressive style as I mentioned earlier. If he is dominating or dictating type the leader would not succeed in retaining the best talent in the organization as people give more importance to self-respect and in the event of not getting self-respect, the subordinates would prefer to leave the organization to avoid conflicts.

3. **Accommodating (9.1):** Here the leader is unassertive and co-operative – exactly the opposite of competing. When the organization/leader offers the best salary, best facilities etc. and loses focus on its goals, one can appreciate, the company would become bankrupt soon as it would function more like a charitable organization which is not good for any business enterprise. Organization can be benevolent only to the extent it can afford and therefore productivity and profitability also need to be given due importance for success of any business.

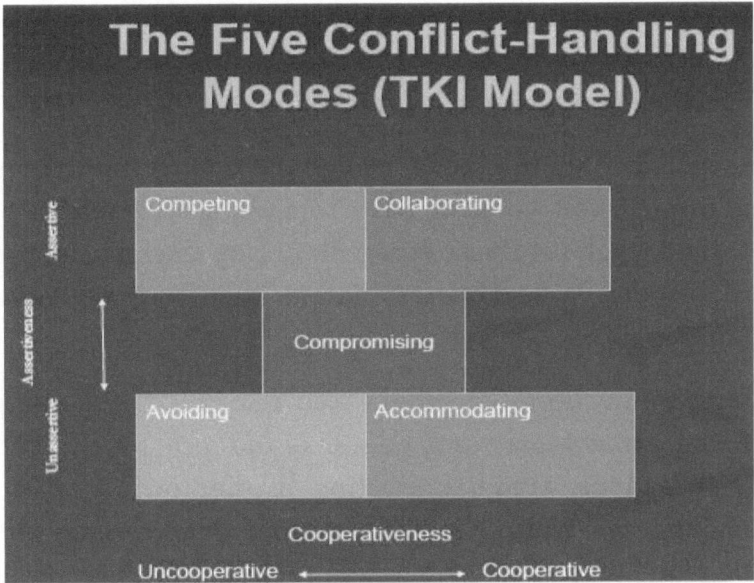

Fig. 5

4. **Compromising (5.5):** This kind of leader is intermediate in both assertiveness and cooperativeness. Compromising falls on a middle ground between competing and accommodating. Here the manager/leader wants to be nice to everyone and tries to maintain good relationship with every individual/group. This may prove to be detrimental to the growth/interest of the organization in the long run as the business would never reach the benchmark levels because the same might have been compromised for maintaining cordial relationship with every group in the organization. In the process, the organization may lose to their competitors which is not a good sign for any healthy organization.

5. **Collaborating (9.9):** Ideally speaking, this is the best one, as it is both assertive and cooperative; a sense of belongingness can be created in the minds of the people because innovative ideas are invited from people who are involved in the ambiguous tasks and they are also empowered to take decisions when situations demands. But collaborating style will be successful only during strategic planning where more time would be available at our disposal. Further, it is needless to mention here that, mutual trust is a must for its success.

We can conclude from the above, though the maximum success can be attained through collaborating style, competing style may also bring in the desired results at times, especially during emergencies provided the leader shows **assertiveness** rather than **aggressiveness** in getting the job done.

In this connection, we should also remember, the competing kind of leader may see accommodator as too nice, overly protective of others' feelings, timid, neglecting his/her own interests and soft-pedalling the truth. Similarly, accommodators may view the competing kind of leader as insensitive to others' feelings, putting his own desires ahead of others, undermining goodwill and trust in the team.

Thus each style has its own merits and demerits and therefore needs to be adopted at the appropriate situation to derive the best results. In this field, the contribution by Robert Blake and Jane Mouton **(The Managerial Grid)** is worth reading (Houston Gulf Publishing 1964, 1994).

Future Leadership

One must admit that all leaders cannot be managers though all managers are expected to be leaders. Leadership of tomorrow will therefore have to focus more on wisdom (a blend of knowledge and experience) and courage than on intelligence and talents. A future leader should have a clear vision of the distant goals and position/power. He must have the dedication, determination, will-power, guts, perseverance, total commitment to his work and the required mental strength for achieving success in his future endeavour. He must strictly follow rules and regulations, adopt policies and procedures by giving values/beliefs to traditions and rituals so as to develop exemplary work culture in the organization. Though he must be flexible to the changing situations, he has to be assertive and stick to his principles forever.

He has to give emphasis on performance and should show ways for its improvement rather than punishments for not performing meticulously. He must make every individual accountable and responsible for the tasks assigned to him/her.

Since one has to be on the learning course always, the leader must encourage creativity and novelty by inviting suggestions, innovative ideas, out of box thinking and participation from his/her peers and subordinates while making/taking decisions which is known as *inclusive leadership style.* He/she must accept the fact that no one is either dependent or independent/indispensable, but they are all inter-dependent while executing a task. One has to remember therefore that any radical reform however well-intentioned may be, can be brought about only by involving others in the formative stage itself as there is bound to be conflict of interests and ideas. For instance, while changing any prevailing practices related to workforce in an organization, it is always better at the outset to consult with the union and take their inputs/views instead of confronting them with a pre-determined decision and expect them to endorse it without any objection or amendment. One will appreciate that it is proper to seek their co-operation and invite their participation so as to achieve the objective of smooth transformation in a more effective manner. HR Managers can act as transformational leaders for bringing about the desired transformation in their organizations by focusing more on opportunities than on tasks and targets, emphasizing more on creativity than on conformities and encouraging employees' involvement and participation in decision making process rather than giving them mere directions. A workable scheme will definitely emerge, if both sides (employees and employer) conduct themselves according to the rules of diplomacy rather than words of war.

One has to remember that when changes are brought to us, they are disturbing, but when they are made by us, the same changes are exhilarating. Hence for the upliftment of an organization or for that matter a nation lies in the essence of leadership that is being followed and its effectiveness on the people especially, when we are talking about economic liberalization and globalization of industries. One will appreciate therefore that it is the prerogative of each individual to groom and encourage a person as leader or CEO (Chief Executive Officer) for an organization who understands the values of life, has problem-solving and decision-making skills and tries to practise what he preaches taking into account the ground realities so as to have a better tomorrow and to help any organization/nation in climbing the pinnacles of success and thereby transcending greater heights.

A successful leader will therefore be one who believes in promoting excellent team-spirit and in converting the weaknesses into strengths after assessing the limitations of his teammates. He will be a definite winner, if he attempts to do things differently instead of doing different things. After all, "Fortune favours the brave" – does it not?

Chapter-10

Safety and Risk Assessment/Management

Safety can be ensured by minimising the risk if not avoiding the same. **Risk Management** has assumed greater significance in recent times, as all tasks (technical or non-technical) involve risks.

Our behaviour pattern, perception and approach to risks matter a lot for safe/flawless operations and therefore all the three elements viz: Behaviour, risk and safety are interrelated and having far reaching consequences. Their impact and effectiveness on one another are delineated in detail in this chapter.

Behaviour ⟶ RISK ⟶ SAFETY

Risk is the likelihood to harm – chance of something adverse happening, uncertainty and lack of knowledge concerning the outcome of the event. The concept of **Risk Management** involves analysing, evaluating and controlling risks which call for identifying hazards (potential problems), evolving control measures – both preventive and corrective actions – so as to ensure safe operations. The latest ISO 9001:2015 focuses more on this aspect especially in the area of corrective and preventive action.

Most of the industrial/road accidents take place because of the following factors:-

- ➢ Lack or inadequacy of – Skill, knowledge, experience or training – all of them lead to incompetency.

- ➢ Lack of confidence or overconfidence-anything in excess always poses as a threat to the quality of performance and productivity.

➢ Casual approach to the problem and lack of commitment on the part of concerned individuals.

➢ Unwillingness to learn from his/her own or others' mistakes. Importance of going through various past case studies should be understood and stressed by making thorough analysis of the same so as to avoid recurrence in future...

➢ Applying short cut methods and Quick-fix solutions by resolving issues at the surface level rather than making root cause analysis of the problems. It is more like giving a cosmetic touch in place of clinical treatment or treating the symptoms rather than the disease itself.

➢ Unwilling to adapt to the changes – in time, technology and situations. We must appreciate change is the only thing which remains constant. We have to accept changes as challenges and opportunities rather than threat because even a small opportunity will provide scope to build a great enterprise in future.

Analysing and Evaluating Risk: Risk basically relates the seriousness of an accident to its frequency. Seriousness refers to the **consequence** of an accident **(C)** and **Frequency** refers to **Probability** of an accident **(F).**

To calculate the risk factor involved in an accident both the elements **viz: Frequency (F) & Consequence (C)** are taken into consideration as both these elements are invariably and inversely proportional to each other.

In other words, whenever the frequency or probability of accidents is higher, the consequence of an accident will be lower.

For example, in a city centre road, where we very often come across heavy traffic especially during peak hours we cannot move fast at high speed however powerful engine you have in your car like BMW etc. because of traffic congestion, frequent red signals or speed limits.

We are in a position to drive at the most @50 km per hour and that too may be for few kilometres only as we have to encounter many traffic signals on our way to work. In view of this, we hardly have any major accidents in city roads especially during peak hours though we meet many minor accidents during that time, as all of us are in a hurry to reach our workplace in time. Under such circumstances, if at all any accident takes place, we may rarely witness any fatal accidents and more than the damage to the persons or to the vehicles the commotion and emotional outburst may be much more than actually warranted.

Further as you know, people including the pedestrians lack discipline and are indiscriminate while crossing roads and hardly observe the traffic rules (viz: using of zebra crossing or subways). Similarly cyclists suddenly take a right turn in a fast moving traffic without showing any sign by his/her hand and in the process if they get hurt if not run over by a heavy vehicle, the public outrage and target will invariably be the driver of the heavy vehicle only, though there was no fault on his/her part. In anticipation and to avert such eventuality people more often use their horns and/or breaks in their vehicles even in the area like hospitals and schools where they are not supposed to do. Thus, the probability of incidents is quite high though its consequence may not be that high.

On the other hand, in a national highway where roads are broader and wider vehicles move very fast (sometimes even @120km per hour) the frequency of accidents is lower as compared to the one which happens in a city roads, but the resultant consequence may be very severe-sometimes even fatal or involves partial/total or permanent disability. People involved in such accidents may so crippled that they may be made to feel that it would have been better had they been rather killed in such accidents so as not to languish their balance period of life. Here as you can understand, the consequence turns out to be more severe.

The risk factor is arrived at by multiplying probability/frequency (F) with Consequence/severity(C).

Risk-factor (RF) = PROBABLITY/FRQUENCY (F) × Consequence (C)
Thus Risk-Factor (RF) = F × C.

Risk factors are broadly divided into 3 Regions/catagories just like having 3 classes in any University Examination results (1st Class, 2nd Class & 3rd Class) namely,

'A' Region = unacceptable

'B' Region = Tolerable

'C' Region = Broadly acceptable

The above mentioned 3 regions may be correlated with the following 3 modes namely,

Evasion mode – which people resort to when they are over confident because of quick reflexes (invariably applicable to the youth) or too much experience (generally seen with the older lots).

Compliance mode – when they strictly adhere to the rules and regulations like following traffic rules while driving.

Safety Mode – Here people are over-cautious and see from others' point of view also.

The same is shown below in the figure (Fig. 1).

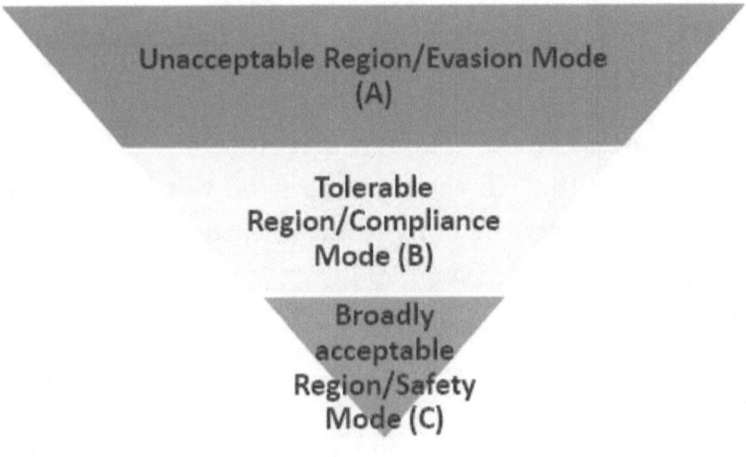

Unacceptable Region/Evasion Mode (A)

Tolerable Region/Compliance Mode (B)

Broadly acceptable Region/Safety Mode (C)

Fig. 1

Thus, the operational risks involved in the case of **(B) and (C)** are minimal but in the case of **(A)** they are at the maximum. Unfortunately people (have the general tendency to) prefer the possible loss to certain inconveniences. For instance, when cargo transfer/or bunker operation is in progress in a vessel and in the event of a sudden deterioration in the weather condition, one has to suspend the operation and take the vessel inside the sea to ensure safety for ship as well as for the involved crews. But to avoid the inconvenience of disconnecting the pipes and reconnecting the same later, the concerned crews (especially if they are more experienced) would continue the operation thinking that it would be finished before the weather gets worse and in the process land themselves into greater problems.

The whole idea of calculating the risk factors is to bring them under **'C'** Region to **A**s **L**ow **A**s **R**easonably **P**racticable (**ALARP** Principle).

This can be made possible by ranking/categorising the risks into the following 5 levels:

5. Intolerable Risks:- Which is neither known nor experienced in the past and may have catastrophic effect like **tsunami** which swept the entire coastal areas in India on **26th December 2004.** Before that date, most people were not even knowing the spelling of **'TSUNAMI.'** Needless to mention here that their awareness of such occurrence was **nil...**

4. Substantial Risk:- Though it is different from Intolerable Risk in the sense that all the persons need not have experienced the catastrophic effect they might have heard of the same through films and other medias. Example: disaster sinking of **Titanic** ship on **14th April 1912** after hitting an iceberg/glacier. Many of us though not experienced the effect of **Titanic** disaster must have at least watched the movie titled **'Titanic'** filmed much later. So the awareness is reasonably good but our experience on this is absolutely nil in most cases.

3. Moderate Risk:- Here the risk is predictable and its effect can be made moderate by acting proactively, taking all the required preventive measures and ensuring that our defence mechanism is stronger. For instance, in a cargo carrying ships (tankers and bulk carriers) you would appreciate, the risk of fire would always be high as they are carrying inflammable liquids & solids and are therefore prone to all sorts of fire accidents. To avert any major fire accidents and to ensure safety to crews, ships keep the extinguishers in place, have designated place for smoking, emergency escape breathing device (EEDP) and life rafts etc. Thus the damage to people and property is minimised if not avoided.

2. Tolerable Risk:- Similarly in ships, the crews may fracture their legs or hands when they have a fall while climbing down from the deck or slipping on a oily floor because of inadequacy of light or lack of proper shoe-grips. The affected persons are to be substituted so that neither the work gets suspended nor the affected persons suffer for want of treatment.

1. Trivial/Negligible Risk:- There is also a possibility of sustaining minor injuries by workers when they are on jobs in a workplace – in the form of small bruises, inflammation in their legs/hands, slight indisposition or irritation in their eyes caused by fumes and dust etc. Under such circumstances, what they need may be a kind of first – aid treatment. Sometimes, in such emergencies, it may so happen that the first-aid box may only be available but there may be no medicines therein or may have medicines which have crossed the expiry date. These kind of issues can be easily resolved if periodical check-up of the stock of medicines are made.

Calculation of Risk Factors for Safety:- By giving due weight-age to both consequence (viz: Nil = 1, Slight = 2, Moderate = 3, High = 4 and Very High = 5) and Frequency/probability (Viz: Highly Unlikely = 1, Unlikely = 2, Moderately Likely = 3, Likely = 4 and Highly Likely = 5) one can arrive at the risk factor (Consequence × Frequency/probability).

As mentioned above, our aim is to bring this down to the **Broadly Acceptable Level ('C' Region)** keeping in view the **ALARP** principle (**A**s **L**ow **A**s **R**easonably **P**racticable principle). In other words, the risk factor (Consequence × Frequency) has to be brought below 4 so as to ensure that they are at the desired acceptable level.

Similarly if the risk factors (Consequence × Frequency) are between 4 & 6 then they are considered to be in the **tolerable Region ('B' Region).**

Needless to mention here that if the risk factors are greater than 6 then they are at **Unacceptable Region ('Á' Region) in a scale of 25 (5 × 5).**

In the event of the risk factor falling under 'A' or 'B' Region necessary control measures need to be taken to bring the same down to 'C' Region.

This number can change with the situation and is dynamic; and therefore would be different for different persons also according to individuals' experience and exposure level.

Nowadays, Risk Assessment forms are designed accordingly in every company/industry. All the concerned individuals have to fill in the form by referring the available check list and the relevant risk library... Then, they need to obtain the necessary approval from their higher authorities before commencing the operation to ensure safety.

It should also be borne in mind that so long everything goes well nobody may check the risk assessment form in detail. However if something goes wrong and in the event of any untoward incident the Pandora's box may be opened and a thorough scrutiny would be made by the appropriate authorities. So, in their own interests the individuals have to fill in the risk assessment form with all seriousness so as not to get themselves into any kind of future trouble.

Safety and Risk Assessment/Management • 103

Further, the objective of introducing Risk Assessment Forms for all operations and insisting the concerned individuals to fill in the same before commencing the operation is to make them accountable as well.

Risk Assessment Techniques:- Following are the 10 different types of risk assessment techniques:-

1. **HAZOP** – Hazard and operability study on equipment – a systematic evaluation of deviations outside the design envelope. The potential for hazard or operability problems exists only when the process deviates outside the design parameters.

2. **Check-list Review** – Use of a list of specific questions to identify the known types of hazards or design deficiencies that may lead to potential accidents or incident scenarios.

3. **So what – If review** – Brainstorming examination of a process, operation or a change to identify potential accidents or incident scenarios and all review generally made at any stage of design, construction or operation of a system or process.

4. **Failure Modes and Effects Analysis (FMEA)** – Component-by-component analysis of system to determine the effects of component failure on the rest of system to ensure sound alternative mechanism for safety.

5. **Job Hazard Analysis** – A procedure to make job safe by identifying the hazards associated with each job step by breaking tasks into sequential steps and developing solutions to each hazard so as to eliminate or control it.

6. A good analogy for accident causation is given by Reason as shown below (please see the Fig. 2). This so-called **Swiss Cheese Model** shows challenges to the safety system as sticks poking through holes in each layer of defence

(these are gaps or deficiencies in each safeguard). If there are insufficient safeguards or – these have too many gaps – then a major accident becomes more likely or inevitable.

Reason's Swiss Cheese Model of Accident Causation

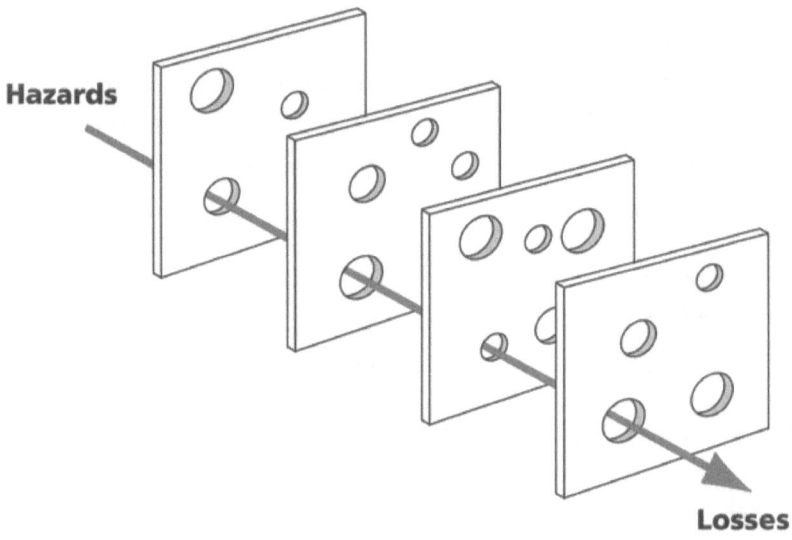

Fig. 2

7. **Change Analysis** – Compare the problem situation to problem-free solution taking into account the time changes, technology changes, personal changes, organizational and operational changes.

8. **Fault tree Analysis** – doing a root cause analysis by considering all possible potential causes and taking all preventive measures so as to avoid the occurrences of such identified problems.

9. **HAZID-Hazard identification** – The primary objectives of which are to identify the potential hazards, be aware of the past accidents by going through various case studies and to allow lateral thinking from diverse experience.

10. **Quantitative Risk Assessment (QRA)** – Whereby a Risk Management Strategy is evolved by calculating the risk considering both frequency and consequence of hazards. The same is depicted through the following flow-chart:

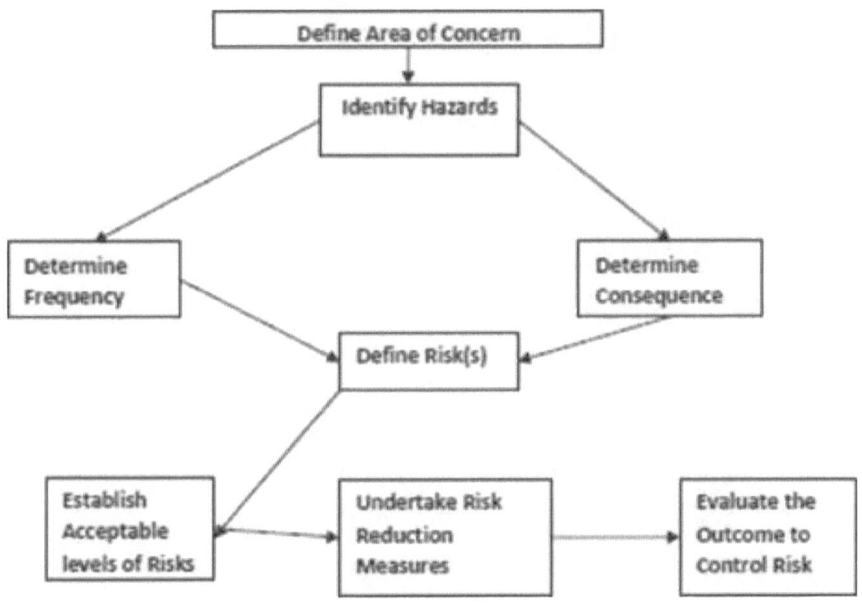

Fig. 3

In conclusion though we have different risk assessment methods and techniques, the main objective is only to ensure safety and safe operation. This can be easily achieved by us if we have the right attitude, diligent approach to the problem so as to give priority to safety.

Acknowledgement:- I place on record my sincere thanks to **Dynacom Tankers Management Limited and also to Oceans XV Nautical services Pvt. Ltd.** for providing valuable inputs related to shipping for this chapter.

This was published as an article in **"Maritime Matrix Today (September 2014 edition)."**

Chapter-11

Behaviour Based Safety Operations – a New Perspective Based on Transactional Analysis

Handling machines and new technology on board ship is not as difficult as handling human beings who are different by nature, culture and behaviour because they originate from different environments. Human behaviour has been one of the major areas of interest and concern for all operations in recent years, especially related to safety. Professionals in all areas are realizing now that their success is influenced by their ability to develop proper interpersonal relations. People of 21st Century therefore need to acquire more people management skills than their predecessors.

One tool that can help improve interpersonal relations is Transactional Analysis (TA). Using TA to understand personality – including our own and how it affects behaviour will help in developing collaborative groups. This, in turn, will improve communication and understanding which are essential to have synergic benefits and for improving safety operations in any organization.

What Is Transactional Analysis (TA)?

Transactional Analysis (TA) can be defined as examining and analysing the communication by breaking into basic units. The unit of social interaction is called **"Transactions." Transactional Analysis (TA)** was originated by Eric Berne (New York) in the year 1964. TA assumes all of us reside in one of three particular mental states (EGO) at all times. The three basic Ego states are as follows:-

1. **Parent Ego:** This ego is specific for every person as it is the direct result of those early experiences in life that are unique to an individual. These experiences are mostly warnings, rules and laws that the child heard/saw from his/her parents The significant point is that, regardless of whether these rules are good or bad, realistic or unrealistic, they are recorded as truths which cannot be erased and have immense influence throughout his/her life... In this state, individual can be either protective and loving or stern and critical. Accordingly the parent ego state can be further classified into two categories:

   ➢ **Critical Parent:** who controls, criticizes and instructs the activity of others.

   ➢ **Nurturing Parent:** In this ego state individual generally helps, supports, protects and encourages others to have a healthy psychological growth.

2. **Child Ego:** The childhood is the most enjoyable part of our life as we move freely without any inhibition, display openness and warmth, respond spontaneously and are generally fun-loving in character. So, when we think, feel, talk and act as we did when we were a little child, we are in our child ego state. During this stage we are dependant, obedient and long for affection and immediate rewards/appreciation for our acts.

3. **Adult Ego:** The adult state is characterized by fairness and therefore considers people as equal and gives them the due respect. The individual gathers relevant information, carefully analyses the same – becomes capable of differentiating the life as was taught to him/her by his/her parent and the life as he/she felt as a child and the life as he/she figures it out himself/herself as an adult with experience and maturity.

The individual concerned generates alternatives and make logical choices. He/she does not act impulsively in a dominating way and approaches the problem in a cool-headed and rational manner while dealing with others.

Importance of Transactional Analysis (TA): TA is important because when you are interacting with your co-workers you can quickly recognize in which ego state they are operating in and then you can adjust your behaviour with the concerned individual accordingly. This will not only optimize the interaction but also enable you to keep the work environment professional and safe. Before understanding the intricacies of various transactions which has a direct impact on the behaviour pattern of the individuals, let us know the meaning of **'Stimulus'** and **'Response.'**

Stimulus – What is done or said to initiate 'Response.'

Response – Behaviour as a result of such 'Stimulus.'

Transactions between Different Ego states

People generally exhibit all three ego states, but one state may dominate the other two. However all three ego states are necessary for a healthy personality but the main aspect is how one ego state compliments or conflicts with another ego state in interpersonal relations. All transactions can be classified under following four categories:-

1. **Complimentary Transaction:** In this case, the **Originator** gets the response in the Ego state that he expects. The **Stimulus** and **Response** lines are parallel to each other.

    Example: Master (Stimulus): 'you are late for your watch again!'

    Third Officer (Response): 'I am sorry, sir.'

In this case, the Master is in the parent state and the third Officer who is in the child state admits his fault and the matter ends there without any conflict.

2. **Crossed Transaction:** In this case, the **Originator** does not get the response in the expected ego state. The **Stimulus** and **Response** lines are not parallel. This can hurt people and can stop or restrict transaction.

   Example: Chief Officer (Stimulus): 'Drain out the tank before you go for lunch. This is very urgent.'

   Second Officer (Response): 'I know my job. You don't have to tell me. I have been doing this for the last five months even before you joined us.'

   Note: It is totally an ineffective transaction. Both of them are in a **parental state** and treat the other person as **child** which is very unhealthy.

3. **Ulterior Transaction:** It involves hidden messages between ego states that are different to what they appear on the surface. As the persons involved are not open to each other this may even cause greater resentments in future.

   Example: Master (Stimulus): 'What is the time now?' (by looking at his watch)

   Second Officer (Response): 'I am sorry for the delay Sir!'

   It may be noted that the Master's response is quite sarcastic. Needless to say, this may strain their relations in future as the Second Officer's ego is hurt because a lot of information is conveyed by the Master through non-verbal cues, by looking at his watch.

4. **Angular Transaction:** This is a variation from the ulterior transaction in which the message of a person is deliberately

expressed in a way that appeals two ego states (Parent & Child ego) on the other. This is done to manipulate/drive home the other person to the desired course of action.

Example: The Designated Person Ashore-DPA (Stimulus): 'This accredited body is the best & is well known worldwide for ISO 9001 Certification. But...... our company cannot afford!'

The Managing Director (MD) (Response): 'We must engage this accredited body for our ISO 9001 Certification.'

Here it can be noted that the Managing Director (MD) would not have gone for the best accredited certification body considering the financial impact on the company, had the DP said that we should go for the best body for ISO 9001 certification. But since he added further after a pause that our company could not afford them it has provoked the MD to accept his suggestion which was his ultimate objective.

Four Life Positions in Transactional Analysis (TA)

This concept brought into focus by **Thomas A Harris** in his best seller **'I am OK-You are OK' (1969).** In this practical guide to TA the following two approaches have been adopted.

How do people view or feel about themselves or others in general?

In each case, there are two possible answers. They are either positive (OK) or negative (Not OK). There are four possible combinations of answers to these questions, which give four possible life positions with respect to self or others. The same are given below:

a. **I am OK-You are not OK**

   - Feels good about self & distrust others.
   - Feels superior to others and operates from **Critical Parent Ego** state.

b. **I am not OK-You are not OK**

   - Personal feelings are negative towards self & others.
   - Distrusts everyone & sees little worth in life and work.

c. **I am not OK-You are OK**

   - Feels inferior to others.
   - always unhappy & needs reassurance and recognition.
   - Operates from **Child Ego** state.

d. **I am OK-You are OK**

   - The most desirable position.
   - Healthy acceptance of self & others.
   - Operates mostly in **Adult** to **Adult** transaction.

Power of Interaction & Communication

Transactional Analysis (TA) enhances the awareness about our own potential while dealing with others on job and enables our decision making process easier. We look at the things as they are, rather than as they ought to be. When such awareness is developed, we not only start listening to others but also to our own inner voice.

We adopt ourselves to changing situations by moving between **Parent, Adult** and **Child** state as per the demands of the situations with the belief that all have the potential for growth.

Managing People: A Leader, a Manager or a Supervisor who can establish an **'I am OK – You are OK'** relationship not only promotes communication and cordial relationship but also encourages creativity to develop both themselves and their team to the fullest. In this context, the following key questions may bring some useful insights and outcome.

- Where is mine and other person's ego state?
- What is he feeling about me and what am I feeling about him?
- Are we hurting each other's ego state?
- Is that what I want?

The inference drawn from the above would not only help us to deal with a Not-OK Child state but also to identify our own Not-OK interpretations.

Needless to say, carrying pre-conceived notions about how others have to behave obstructs in building relationships. One has to be honest to oneself and with others. For developing congenial working environment mutual trust is a must which would ensure continual improvement for any operation.

SWOT Analysis: Finally, another tool which can be useful in our operation is carrying out **S**trengths, **W**eaknesses, **O**pportunities **& T**hreats **(SWOT)** analysis of any situation so that we will not only improve our strengths and overcome our weaknesses but also would be in a position to distinguish between the opportunities and threats. More often than not we consider opportunities as threats and threats as opportunities and in the process we land ourselves in greater problems.

Example: The master of a vessel refuses the third officer's request to see a dentist in a U.S. Gulf port as it would be rather expensive. On passage to Venezuela the third officer's condition becomes worse and he is unable to keep sea watches.

Eventually he has to be airlifted off to Curacao. This is a classic case of missing an opportunity considering the same as a threat.

Safe operations can be ensured only when we are able to identify the difference between the opportunities and threats. This enables us to take decisive actions under any circumstances.

Post script: By using the tools of **MYERS-BRIGGS TYPE INDICATORS (MBTI) & 16PF (16 Personality Factors)** one can assess his own personality and his teammates as well. The tools are available free on www.personalityperfect.com and www.psychometrictest.org.uk/16pf-test.

Chapter-12

Beyond Politics to People

Organization Politics is inevitable and is a necessary evil. The role of Human Resources in dealing such crucial issues is pivotal.

The HR Manager has to appreciate his/her role well – though s/he should neither play nor create politics but resolve matters amicably keeping in view the organizational interests and without any prejudice. Bigger the organisation greater the consequences and repercussions because of various conflicts of interests and therefore the HR Manager has to act as a facilitator in reaching consensus.

Reason for conflicts:- Internal politics in the working world arises because of the prevalence of the following seven toxins in excess:-

- **Complaints**
- **Criticism**
- **Gossips**
- **Backbiting**
- **Jealousy**
- **Interference**
- **Ego clashes**

All the above are indicators of the absence of openness and transparency which would result in unhealthy atmosphere. One has to learn to admire but not envy, to follow but not imitate, to praise but not flatter, to lead but not force, to manoeuvre but not to be manipulative so as to avoid any negative vibration in the working environment.

How to Manage the Workplace Toxins?

- **Complaint** is nothing but an expression of a grievance and in short, an accusation. Why a person makes a complaint-because of mental or physical disturbance caused by others. It is quite possible sometimes that the perception of the person who makes the complaint may be incorrect as well. In all cases HR Manager plays an important role in resolving the issue. S/he should give a patient hearing of both sides initially on one to one basis on receiving a verbal/written complaint, afterwards do the necessary counselling, try to understand their viewpoints separately and later on collectively call them to explain each other's position. Finally, HR Manager has to suggest the best possible solution to remove all misgivings, to protect the interest of the aggrieved party and to resolve the matter once for all.

- **Criticism** means finding faults, pointing out, analysing and evaluating the merits and demerits of facts. The HR Head has to find out the objective of the person/Division who makes the criticism about the other. If the aim is cynical and only to find faults and not to find facts then it is detrimental to the organization and hence to be weeded out at the first instance so as to avoid any ill-effects. On the other hand, if the aim is to highlight certain facts then the approach of the HR Head should be positive and to encourage all constructive suggestions to make all possible improvements.

- **Gossips...** Indulge in idle and mischievous talks (by people who cannot find anything better to do), usually about the affairs and personal life of others which are purely non-productive. The main aim is not to prove a point but to disprove others, generally to degrade and belittle others which are always unnecessary and to be nipped at the bud through

HR interventions so as not to pollute the surroundings and to ensure exemplary work culture.

- **Backbiting...** Making a verbal attack on some people behind their backs when they are not around to defend themselves. This reflects only the person's lack of courage in facing the concerned persons directly. It is similar to gossip, but more malicious and with more evil intent. It generally indicates a personal vendetta, a private ware-fare or feud which is directed toward a particular person or persons. Since the motive is ulterior the HR interventions on such issues is crucial so that ii would not antagonize the organization's team-spirit.

- **Jealousy...** Resentfulness and hostile envy toward someone because of their advantages and good fortune. Sometimes healthy disregard is fine but in most cases the concerned persons have grudging respect and total mistrust with each other which affects the day to day affairs of the organization. The HR Head has to bring this to their notice so as to emphasize the importance of team work.

- **Interference** is to obstruct the process, meddle and intervene in other areas of operations to show their importance and superiority which will impede and hinder progress and therefore to be discouraged by framing suitable HR Policies to draw the bottom-line viz: *lakshman-rekha*. We must remember, one can give his/her ideas only when it is sought after and not otherwise, however well-intentioned it may be.

- **Ego clashes** are the reflection of the personality tussle and most of the times the conflicts arise because the concerned individuals are self-centred and tend to take things too personally rather than handling the same professionally. Such persons are more concerned about their own position in the organization than about the organization they serve. We must remember no one in the organization is bigger than the organization regardless of his/her position in the organization. Such persons may hinder even in implementing development oriented projects just to show their importance and power. They may raise certain trivial objections just for the sake of objecting. They must realize, no one in the organization is indispensable and may be spared in pursuit of achieving the organizational goals. After all, business is always different from businessman and this has to be borne in mind in the right perspective.

Difficulty in saying 'Yes' or 'No':- More often than not people accept or reject proposals not on the basis of its merits but on their personal liking/disliking of the persons from whom they receive such proposals. Proposals need to be considered purely on its merits regardless of the persons who have made the same. Sometimes we have difficulty in saying **"No"** to certain persons just because we do not want to displease them because of their age, experience and position. Similarly, we have problems in saying **"Yes"** as well, when someone reposes confidence in us and in our potentials thereby gives additional responsibility. We shy away from taking the responsibilities considering the same, as additional burden and threats rather than challenges and opportunities and bluntly refuse to accede to their proposal. Ideally speaking, balancing act would be to extend issue based support rather than making the same too much personalized. Saying **'Yes or No'** should have valid reasons and to be supported by logics. 'This would not only give immense satisfaction to all but also would provide fruitful results and ensure *win-win situation.*

The Role of Human Resources:- The HR Head has to understand and differentiate the above toxins, its implications and intricacies well. S/he must realize that most of them are related to attitudinal problems of people and hence to be dealt judiciously by finding ways and means to provide appropriate solutions so as to safeguard the interests of the people in general and the organization in particular. S/he should know, how to make use of **Kipling's 5 Ws-What, When, Who, Where and Why** – to divulge and to **whom and how,** so as to ensure effective results for the organization. S/He should not only act as a conduit and an able communicator but also be a good listener. We must bear in mind ability to listen is much more important and difficult than ability to communicate. Once HR Head has his/her role clarity well, s/he can act as a true enabler for a winning organization by setting aside all petty politics.

Chapter-13

Managing Stress

Stress is the psychological and physiological response to events that upset our personal balance in some way. These events or demands are known as stressors. Workplace stress has negative impact on the individual-employee. The increase in job stress creates emotional, financial and safety concerns for employees/employers and managers. The World Health Organization (WHO) labeled stress as a **'worldwide epidemic'** which needs to be eradicated.

The main reason for our stress is our inability to accept the reality. When something is happening or about to happen not the way we want and we accept it, it becomes tolerance and when we don't accept it, it causes us to get angry. In this connection I would like to share here some beautiful answers and way of thinking of Turkish poet Jalaluddin Rumi, which are given below:-

'What Is Fear??' – when we encounter uncertainties and we don't accept such uncertainties, it causes fear to us.

According to him, non-acceptance of uncertainty causes fear. If we accept that uncertainty, it becomes **Adventure.**

'What is jealous/envy??' – non-acceptance of good in others makes us to feel jealous. If we accept that good qualities in others, it becomes **Inspiration** for us.

When somebody has something which we don't have or somebody is able to produce results which we are not able to do so and we refuse to accept that fact we become jealous of him/her. When we accept that reality, we try to study his/her life, get inspired and thereby learn how it can be humanly made possible through perseverance.

'What is hatred??' – non-acceptance of a person as he/she is, leads to hatred. If we accept a person unconditionally, we start loving him/her.

Lastly, when he was asked, 'what is poison?' he replied with a beautiful answer – anything which is more than our necessity is **Poison.** It may be Power, Wealth, Hunger, Ego, Greed, Laziness, Love, Ambition, Hate, or anything.

In short, one needs to be needy and not to be greedy so as to lead stress-free life.

Factors Lead to Job Stress

1. **Excessive work load:** We must appreciate, high work load, tedious or meaningless tasks, long hours and low pay, unreasonable performance demands and infrequent rest/breaks at the work place may all lead to high stress. That is why, the international requirements stipulate 77 hours of rest per week for any worker (an average of 11 hours per day) to recuperate from physical and mental fatigue. Needless to mention here that proper work-life balance is a must to reduce the stress level. It should also be kept in mind here, low work load may also sometimes lead to stress because empty mind is devil's nest. It is essential therefore to ensure effective use of available human power is a must to have a high productive organization.

2. **Physical work environment:** Awareness on **'Environmental consciousness'** has increased ever since **ISO 14001** has been enforced (1996) globally to ensure safe working environment/surroundings. Noise pollution, poor air quality, over-crowding, toxic chemicals etc. contribute to all stress related issues.

3. **Organizational Practices:** Conflicting job demands, prevalence of unclear and overlapping of responsibilities in organizations may increase the stress levels of individuals.

Further, multiple supervisors and lack of autonomy or participation in decision making and inefficient/ineffective communication are the causes for concern as they are the major contributing factors for stress in any organization which should be kept in mind while framing policies by the top management.

4. **Career Development/advancement:** Here the Maslow's law and Herzberg's two-factor theory of motivation play an important role to develop a positive attitude among people in any working environment. People's attitude will remain positive if we identify and fulfil their needs and expectations. In this connection, we must remember, different people have different needs and same people have different needs at different times because their priorities get changed according to the time. Initially, when a person joins an organization, he/she thinks about salary and job security which are the basic needs for any individual. As he/she works for few years and gains experience his/her focus get shifted towards career growth and advancement. If timely promotion is not given he/she looks for career opportunities elsewhere as he/she develops a feeling that he/she is being exploited by the present organization which may lead to stress in view of the fact that his/her contribution goes unnoticed despite the earnest efforts on his/her part which is not a healthy sign for any developing organization. This aspect has to be kept in mind by the top management to retain the best talents. Because more than recruiting the best talents retaining them and offering career opportunities for growth/need-based training are equally important for any growing organization; otherwise, it may adversely affect organizational environment/interests leading to restlessness and tension among people.

5. **Work place change:** We must appreciate change is inevitable and the only thing which remains constant. We have to

accept changes as challenges and opportunities rather than threats, as small opportunities are always the beginning of a great enterprise. But unfortunately, only people who welcome changes are babies with wet diapers as they cause discomforts to them and all others resist changes because they don't want to come out of their comfort zone. As time changes, technology also changes and therefore we need to be on the learning course always. If anybody glorifies the past, it means he is not comfortable with the present. We must remember, past is history and future is mystery and present is only gift and that is why it is called **"Present."** So, neither we should brood over the past nor worry about the future much; instead, we should remain focused on the present to ensure a better future. In other words, we need to be proactive rather than reactive to avoid stress. In this regard, a small story is narrated below to emphasize the point:

A professor holding a glass of water in his hand asked his students, "How heavy is the glass of water?"

One student said, "It must be around 250 grams!"

Another student retorted by saying, "It should be 300 grams!" and the third one claimed that it should be at least 350 grams.

The professor responded to the class by saying that the absolute weight of the glass did not matter but, it all depended on how long one held on the glass in his hand. If anyone held on to it for a minute or two nothing would happen to him/her. However, if he/she held on to it for an hour or two, we would appreciate that the arm would begin to ache. Needless to say that when we held on to it for the whole day our arms would feel numb and might even be paralyzed. So, longer we hold on the glass heavier we would feel though the weight of the glass has not changed. He added further by saying that the stress and worries in our life are more like a glass of water. If we worry about our problems for a while nothing would happen. But if we worry a little longer we might feel heavier as it would begin to hurt us and when we think all day long about our problems, we might even feel crippled and incapable of doing anything as they would become the real obstacles and prevent us from doing things. Therefore to have a stress-free life we must learn to put the glass/our worries down at the earliest to face the challenges in our life.

Here comes the importance of people's attitude – whether a glass is half-full or half-empty depends on the attitude of the person looking at it. If one says it is half-full that means he/she is optimistic in his/her views. But if he/she says, it is half empty it indicates his/her views are pessimistic. The person with an HR background would neither say half-full nor half-empty. He/she would always say that the glass is too big or too small for its contents as his/her views would be realistic. So, one needs to be realistic in his/her approach to problems in life to lead an easy going and stress-free life.

6. **Interpersonal relationships:** Maintaining good interpersonal relationships at the workplace is very important to avoid any personality tussles and to ensure healthy and friendly work environment. Office politics, unhealthy competitions among work groups, ego clashes and other conflicts are the real causes of concern for stress among people. In this connection we have to remember the following:

   a. Blaming others means lack of education which is mainly because feeling superior to others and is reflection of the existence of **parent ego.**

   b. Blaming oneself means feeling inferior and indicates that education has just started.

c. Neither blaming self nor others means education is complete – which is the indication of the prevalence of **adult ego** and is the most desirable for any healthy organization.

Therefore while recruiting people for an organization, Emotional Quotient (EQ) is more emphasized and given more priority than Intelligent Quotient (IQ) in order to ensure impulse control among people and to maintain harmony at the workplace.

7. **View of the situation:** We all must appreciate, **"Circumstances do not disturb us, but our view of the circumstances disturbs us a lot which ultimately causes stress to us."** In this regard, the following inspiring story will explain, how our view of things would affect/or have a positive effect on our life:-

A famous writer was in his study room. He picked up his pen and started writing:-

** Last year, I had a surgery and my gall bladder was removed. I had to stay stuck to the bed due to this surgery for a long time.

** The same year I reached the age of 60 years and had to give up my favourite job. I had spent 30 years of my life in this publishing company.

** The same year I experienced the sorrow of the death of my father.

** And in the same year my son failed in his medical exam because he had a car accident. He had to stay in bed at a hospital with the cast on for several days. The destruction of car was another loss.

At the end he wrote: Alas! It was such a bad year!!

When the writer's wife entered the room, she found her husband looking sad and lost in his thoughts. From behind his back she read what was written on the paper. She left the room silently and came back with another paper and placed it on side of her husband's writing.

When the writer saw that paper, he found his name written on it with the following lines:-

** Last year I finally got rid of my gall bladder due to which I had spent years in pain...

** I turned 60 with sound health and got retired from my job. Now I can utilize my time to write something better with more focus and peace......

** The same year my father, at the age of 95, without depending on anyone or without any critical condition met his Creator...

** The same year, God blessed my son with a new life. My car was destroyed but my son stayed alive without getting any disability.

At the end she wrote:

This year was an immense blessing of God and it passed well!!

The writer was indeed happy and amazed at such beautiful and encouraging interpretation of the happenings in his life in that year!!!

Moral of the story: In our daily lives, we must realize that it is not happiness that makes us grateful but gratefulness that makes us happy.

Therefore, we have to think positive always to stay happy in our life. We must also remember to be empathetic rather than sympathetic while dealing with people. In other words, we must learn to see things from others' point of view to understand them better and act as an enabler/facilitator in resolving their issues rather than doing their job by ourselves. For instance, an officer has to help his subordinates by giving them the required tools, providing them training etc. to enable them to perform their jobs better rather than doing their jobs to improve productivity and reduce their stress. Needless to mention here, if an officer does the job of his workers who will do his jobs for which he is being paid by the organization? It must be borne in our mind always that wastage of time by individuals (internal factors and controllable by self) may always cause stress though loss of time due to reasons beyond our control (external factors) may not necessarily be a cause for our concern/stress.

8. **Job related and Organizational specific stressors:** Economic conditions, market & technological changes, competition, changes in the production & products/product development, drive for greater cost effectiveness, mergers & acquisitions/change in ownerships are all contributing factors for causing stress to employees as these all act as threats for their job security. In view of the above factors, the management would prefer to have flatter organization which may lead to change in the organization structure and adoption of situation based leadership style which in turn would result in change in the reward system and promotion policies. The message for the employees would be clear – **"Perform or Perish."** This may cause fear psychosis among employees however efficient he/she may be and the very fear of losing their jobs may lead to their mental stress and depression as everyone would be made to feel surplus/unwanted. Apart from the above, the demographic characteristics of population (such as age, competency income etc.) in a family or in an organisation/nation may also be a contributing factor for stress if it is proved to be a liability rather than a dividend.

9. **Problems related to Family:** Loss of spouse or death of any close relatives, marital problems including separation/divorce, major health problems for self or any of the family members may all cause tremendous stress. Needless to mention, financial difficulties in view of the above problems may drain out anyone both mentally & physically. In such

precarious circumstances, time is the best healer and therefore one needs to be patient and avoid any drastic steps so as to avert any further serious aggravation and distress.

10. **Behavioural Symptoms:** We have the tendency not to displease/disappoint anyone and in the process we place ourselves under unwanted pressure by setting unrealistic targets which may ultimately lead to stress. We must learn to say **'No'** if it is not possible for us to do by giving reasons. We must appreciate, saying **'No'** and not doing is always better than saying **'Yes'** and not able to fulfil our commitments as we are likely to disappoint them more by not completing in time thereby losing their trust & faith on us. Needless to mention here that our inability to meet the demands in our jobs would shatter our confidence levels. We need to make **SWOT** (**S**trengths, **W**eakness, **O**pportunities and **T**hreats) analysis so as to make our decision making process easier; we have to improve our strengths, overcome the weakness and learn to distinguish between opportunities and threats so that we do not suffer from any mental or physical disorder which in turn would help us in leading an overwhelming life.

Symptoms of stress: Stress can be easily felt by the following symptoms:-

- Intellectual symptoms which may be in the form of – memory problems, difficulty in making decisions, confused or perplexed state of mind, poor judgment and tendency to run away from problems mainly due to lack of courage etc. – which all can affect our mind.

- Emotional symptoms – hypersensitive, anxiety, depression, getting irritated on filthy issues, lack of confidence, anger and resentment etc. – which are indicative of our feeling.

- Physical symptoms – headaches, digestive problems, fatigue, chest pain or irregular heartbeat, sleep disturbances, high blood pressure, weight loss or gain, decreased sex drive etc. – which directly affect our body.

- Behavioural symptoms – eating disorder, loosing temper, isolating self from others (living in a shell), increasing use of alcohol/cigarettes, nervous habits like nail biting/teeth grinding/jaw clenching, neglecting others, neglecting responsibilities etc.

Needless to mention, if such symptoms go unnoticed and are allowed to be prolonged it may lead to all kinds of major health problems like heart attacks, kidney failure, ulcers, thyroid problems etc.

Stress on the job creates high cost to the business as it affects the morale, productivity and earnings of the organizations to a great extent. It is therefore very much essential to reduce the workplace stress as much as possible keeping in view the best interests of everyone (both employer and employees).

Stress reduction techniques: It is noteworthy that many stress reducing techniques have yielded best results and brought about total transformation in our everyday life. Let us now describe those aspects in detail which we do hope, would help individuals and organizations as a whole to a great extent.

Organizational approach: The first step towards solving the problem is to begin the process and procrastination has to be avoided. Organizations can foster low levels of job stress and high levels of productivity by making use of the following tools for effective results:-

- Introduce and encourage two-way effective communication to develop a friendly social climate, to involve employees in decisions and thereby give them a feeling that they are being heard and part of the team/organization.

- Call for brainstorming to find solutions and to invite new/innovative ideas/suggestions.

- Offer rewards and incentives for their best suggestion to bring about turnaround in the organization.

- Define job descriptions/responsibilities and offer scope for job enrichment for employees.

- Adopt situation based leadership styles viz: autocratic/directive style during emergencies, supportive for repetitive, monotonous, laborious and voluminous work, participative style while handling peers & democratic style when dealing with people involved in non-repetitive, ambiguous and innovative tasks. This will surely keep the spirits of the organization and people high.

- Delegate tasks and break-up big projects by establishing process steps wherever needed.

- Give emphasis on periodical and need-based training to individuals which not only enhance their competencies but also provide opportunities for career advancement/development.

- Provide recreation facilities for employees and their families for relaxation after office/working hours to enable them to recharge themselves and reduce fatigue. We can appreciate all the above steps will motivate the employees and keep their morale high.

Stress Interview: The organization should also ensure at the time of recruiting people for position which involves high amount of stress by conducting stress interview. This technique is generally adopted when candidates are applying for jobs/positions involves considerable pressure such as – Industrial Relations (IR) Manager for union negotiations, Sales Managers for meeting high sales targets overcoming all hurdles in a cut throat competition. The candidates are put under severe emotional strain by rapid firing of questions at the time of interview to test their response. An unfriendly atmosphere is purposely is made by the interviewers to make them uncomfortable to check their reactions. The potential candidates are even asked to wait for 2 to 3 hours at the lobby before the actual interview to test their patience and commitment. But caution has to be exercised in this technique of selection as it may misfire and we may sometimes lose the best candidates also. In order to get the best results, it is essential to ensure that such interviews are conducted by the trained psychologists who know how to hold such interviews.

Individual approach: Change of lifestyle habits helps us to manage stress better. Following practices would help us to improve our quality of life to a great extent:-

- Switch off the office/work place worries the moment we leave for home daily and vice-versa to maintain proper work-life balance.

- Going to sleep early and get adequate sleep (7 to 8 hours a day).

- Involve yourself in some sports activities of your choice; enjoy yourself by listening to music and play instruments which are real stress busters.

- Socializing with people around.

- Do exercise regularly (at least brisk walking for 2 to 3 miles daily) to keep ourselves fit and active.

- Learn the art of breathing exercise, meditation and yoga from a competent person which would help us to remain focused and relaxed always.

- Eat a balanced and nutritious food & have dinner at least 3 hours before going to sleep.

- Reduce caffeine and alcohol intake as it harms our health & gives only temporary reliefs rather than offering any permanent solutions to our problems in the long run.

- Improve our Emotional Quotient (EQ) as we grow older/up in our career apart from Intelligent Quotient (IQ) which will help us to enhance our impulse control.

- Learn to control ourselves rather than trying to control others.

- Have control over our thought processes by bringing in change in ourselves before attempting to change others.

- Accept the things which we cannot change, have the courage to change things which we can and acquire the wisdom to distinguish between the two.

- Accept changes as challenges and opportunities rather than threats.

- Always remember, if we fail to plan means we are planning to fail.

- Prioritize our work and learn to manage our time well as it cannot be recovered again once it is lost.

- Do one thing at a time and learn the art of **Time Management.**

- To make progress in our life, we must learn to compare with ourselves and not with others as comparing with others would only make us feel jealous and ruin our peace.

- Manage our **ANGER** which is one letter short of the word **DANGER** (match stick has a head and not a brain and once it is struck with a matchbox we know it would flare up). Whenever we get angry/upset with someone it is preferable to hold our temper and move away from the place as neither argument nor criticism is going to help anyone.

- Remember, when we shout at someone it means we are feeling far away from him/her by heart, however closely we may be by distance which is not a good sign and may only increase our stress levels. Whenever we have complaints/grievances against someone/situation or have a fight with anyone, we actually put poison in our system. It ranges from small dose to maximum dose of poison-irritation is a small dose, mental disturbance is a little higher dose, frustration is much higher dose and anger is the highest dose of poison. And if we feel like taking a revenge/vengeance against anyone, it is more like drinking the poison directly in huge quantity. This poison is the real cause for all our diseases viz: headache, blood pressure, diabetes, ulcer, cancer etc. which ultimately do not make our life at ease. In fact all diseases keep us at **dis-ease** which means lack of ease or harmony within our body. So do not hold onto **anger** and try to come out of it as quickly as possible to lead a blissful life.

- Learn to say **Thank you** and **Sorry** instantly wherever needed without any reservations.

- Learn to say **NO** and hear **NO** by assessing and appreciating the situations.

- Set realistic targets always and keep improving the same year after year on continual basis.

Effect of Stress reducing techniques/intervention: In nutshell, we can conclude that what we really need is to change our attitude towards life and problems because attitude (behaviour pattern) and not mere aptitude (skills and knowledge) determines the altitude of our life. We should not look for perfection in everything though we need to work towards perfection which is an on-going process in our life. All our activities are part of a process which has one or more objectives. We have to follow the process steps as each process has both inputs and outputs. Therefore it is essential on our part to ensure that no short cut methods are adopted as it may lead to short-circuits. Performance indicators need to be identified and established for each process in order to have control and to ensure continual improvements.

We therefore need to be clear in our thought process and remember the following:-

- Life is a mystery to be lived and not a problem to be solved.
- Life is not a problem to be solved, but a reality to be experienced- both quoted by Soren Kierkegaard (Danish Philosopher of 19th Century).
- Comprehend the definition of life which is the reflection of our thoughts.
- Thoughts can be expressed through words.
- Words can be shown through actions.
- Repeated actions will become our habits.
- Habits will show our character which would ultimately determine our destiny.

So, with a bad attitude we can never have a positive day, however with a positive attitude we can never have a bad day.

Let us try to lead a wonderful and stress-free life always.

Post script: The **Social Readjustment Rating Scale (SRRS)** designed in the year 1967 by psychiatrists, Thomas Holmes and Richard Rahe is given in the following page to evaluate our stress levels. The scale measures stress in **Life Change Units (LCU)**.

Measuring the Potential Impact of Change on Health

The Social Readjustment Rating Scale, designed in 1967 by psychiatrists, Thomas Holmes and Richard Rahe, evaluates the stress levels of important life changes (both planned and unplanned) and correlates them with illness. The scale measures stress in Life Change Units (LCU) and has been used in hundreds of studies on life change and illness onset.

To measure your stress according to the Holmes and Rahe Stress Scale add the number of "Life Change Units" that apply to events you experienced in the past year. If the event occurred more than once, multiply that number by the life change units. The cumulative score will give a rough estimation of your potential risk for illness.

Life event	Life change units	Life event	Life change units
Death of a Spouse	100	Trouble with in-laws	29
Divorce	73	Outstanding personal achievement	28
Marital separation	65	Spouse starts or stops work	26
Imprisonment	63	Begin or end school	26
Death of a close family member	63	Change in living conditions	25
Personal injury or illness	53	Revision of personal habits	24
Marriage	50	Trouble with boss	23
Dismissal from work	47	Change in working hours or conditions	20
Marital reconciliation	45		

Life event	Life change units	Life event	Life change units
Retirement	45	Change in residence	20
Change in health of family member	44	Change in schools	20
Pregnancy	40	Change in recreation	19
Sexual difficulties	39	Change in church activities	19
Gain a new family member	39	Change in social activities	18
Business readjustment	39	Minor mortgage or loan	17
Change in financial state	38	Change in sleeping habits	16
Change in frequency of arguments	35	Change in number of famil reunions	15
Major mortgage	32	Change in eating habits	15
Foreclosure of mortgage or loan	30	Vacation	13
Change in responsibilities at work	29	Christmas	12
Child leaving home	29	Minor violation of law	11

Source: http://en.wikipedia.org/wiki/Holmes_and_Rahe_stress_scale

Studies show a modest correlation between the number of life change units experienced in the previous year with a person's health in the present year.

Interpretation of Your Score

≥ **300: high risk of Illness.**

150–299: moderate risk of Illness.

< 150: reduced risk of illness.

Please Note: This self-assessment tool provides only a rough estimation of your risk for illness as correlated with your stress level. An Individual s response to life events can vary greatly from one person to another and factors such as personality, coping strategies, lifestyle, and availability of resources also alter the effect the siluation has on health and risk of illness.

When "change happens" in your life, we hope you'll implement the strategies discussed in the webinar to help you move through life's challenges with greater ease and confidence and reduce your risk of illness.

References:

Richard Rahe's website: www.drrahe.com. (Revised and updated "Life Changes Stress Test" and "Stress and Coping Inventory" tools are available for a small fee).

T.H. Holmes and R.H. Rahe, "The Social Readjustment Rating Scale," *Journal Psychosomatic Research* 11(2):213-B, 1967.

Chapter-14

The Rise & Fall of Human Power

"Great Ability develops and reveals itself increasingly with every New Assignment."

– **Baltasar Gracian (Spanish Philosopher)**

There are three types of people:

1. Those who make things happen,
2. Those who watch things happen, &
3. Those who wonder what happened.

The first category people are obviously great indeed who achieve their desired, distant but distinct results in life by design and not by default. They believe in themselves, acquire knowledge and share the same with others for effective utilization and benefits. They neither negotiate out of fear nor do they fear to negotiate as they know that courage is not the absence of fear but overcoming of the fear. They display a great deal of character and patience even during the periods of adversity.

According to Edwin C. Bliss **'Success is not the absence of failures; it means attainment of ultimate objectives. It means winning the war, not every battle.'** So, one has to remain focused always in life if his/her vision and mission need to be fulfilled.

State of mind and Facts of life: In hindsight, we can realize that we learn more from our mistakes and failures than from our success as we often overlook our shortcomings and never try to overcome the same during our period of success. On the other hand, when we fail in our attempts to achieve our goals, we try to do an introspection and analysis so as to avert the recurrences of slips, lapses and mistakes in future which were unintentionally committed. The underlying issue under any given circumstances is how we cope up and sustain the pressure both during the period of success and crisis/failure. In the quest of climbing the pinnacles of success we should never resort to any violations and should aim to peak on a high note through the fairest means so as to be remembered ever for our good deeds. Otherwise, any short cut methods will lead to short circuits and end us up to a great fall rather than windfall.

Paradox of success and failures: More often than not, we may have the following **ACE** factors because of repetitive success:-

1. **A**pathy – not showing concerns to others' problems, remaining indifferent and arrogant and insensitive to others' feelings.

2. **C**omplacency-looses urge for further growth.

3. **E**go – suffers from superiority complex and parent ego which makes one to remain self-centred and boastful. S/he carries a false hypothesis that prevents him/her from listening to others and the warning signals-irrespective of the realities.

We always have the tendency to prefer a possible loss to certain inconvenience regardless of the seriousness of the loss just because we have got away with it scot-free on earlier occasions.

On the other hand, during the periods of adversity we do not get the required support as others do not repose confidence in us (in spite of our earlier success in the past) which makes us dejected and inferior at times that ultimately affects our performance further.

We would do a world of good to a person who suffers from failures if we help them know their weaknesses & strengths and also assist them to overcome their weaknesses and develop their strengths further rather than disdaining them. The first step towards success is made if one realizes one's weaker spots even before others come to know about the same so that s/he can act freely without any inhibitions or hindrances. Sooner we realize our mistakes and learn a lesson from such experience is better for us. The ultimate objective of a person in life is to devise ways and means to convert oneself from unconsciously incompetent stage to consciously competent level. The fact is that some of us may take months while others may spend their whole span of life to achieve this objective.

The **'Transactional Analysis'** helps the people in understanding their own ego states and those of the others. It also enables them to interact in more meaningful ways with one another. You may kindly refer Chapter 11 (Behaviour Based Safety Operations) to understand the same in detail. Similarly, the Cause-effect and the root-cause analysis would not only help us in identifying the causal factors and potential problems but also guide us in taking the remedial measures to avoid recurrences/occurrences.

Changes and challenges: Changes and metamorphosis are inevitable in life. People who refuse to accept the changes either blame others (aggressiveness) or blame themselves (submissiveness). In fact, the situations do not disturb them but their views of the situations disturb them. Unless we learn the art of adjusting ourselves to changes so as to bring about the required transformation within ourselves there is no scope for individual growth. To attain growth, one needs to be assertive & forthright and to consider changes as challenges and opportunities rather than threats.

Persons who upgrade their competencies (ability and desire to apply what is learned) from time to time through self-study and self-talk to keep abreast of the latest techniques will be able to adopt themselves to the changing situations and thereby will have greater scope for growth & success in life.

Balancing act in Life: In fact in the present day competitive world, people experience pressure both during periods of success and failures. When they are successful they are worried whether they would maintain the same consistently and live up to the expectations of others forever.

On the other hand, when people repeatedly fail, they desperately try their level best to have a breakthrough so as to come out of the jinx. We must bear in mind that neither success nor failure should disturb anybody as nothing is permanent in life and therefore we have to take both of them in our strides in the right perspective and maintain equanimity and balance always.

If this cardinal aspect is understood well by us, we can face any challenges boldly and would be a definite winner in our professional and personal life.

Mr. Mark Twain has said, **'Twenty years from now you will be more disappointed by the things you didn't do than by the ones you did.'**

So, let us unleash our natural instincts as they may reward us with remarkable results sooner than we imagine.

Chapter-15

Institution Building: Individual vs. Social Responsibility

"We cannot always build the future for our youth, but we can build our youth for the future."

– Franklin D. Roosevelt
(Thirty-Second US President 1933–1945)

We all appreciate that different individuals have different needs and even the same individual may have different needs to be met at different times. As per Maslow's Law of Motivation, needs of individuals are broadly classified as – (a) basic Needs *viz:* food and *shelter*, (b) Safety and Security Needs (both these needs are known as hygiene factors as per Herzberg theory of Motivation), (c) Esteem and Status Needs-*viz:* ego, status, timely recognition and career advancement and (d) Self-actualization Needs-*viz:* Responsibility, achievements and fulfilment (both (c) and (d) are known as higher levels of needs as per Herzberg's theory of Motivation). Thus, every individual has certain targets in his/her mind and so do the organizations/institutions have with whom one is associated. To achieve his/her own individual targets one involves himself/herself in fulfilling the organizational/Institutional goals. Needless to mention here that once the individuals' targets are met the Institutional goals are also automatically met and *vice-versa*. This is where and how both Individual and Social responsibility come in the picture.

Individual responsibility refers to accountability to self and family by not abdicating his/her duties; whereas Social responsibility reflects one's total commitment to render service to society/Institution to which s/he is attached. If our aim is to serve the Society, our claim to our people must be to "act locally and think globally" in institution building by demonstrating "Simple Living and High Thinking." The primary objective of this chapter is not only to accentuate this fact but also to show the ways and means of achieving the same by displaying commitment at all levels.

Each one of us wants to give back something to our family and the Society with which we are attached to, so as to get a feeling of satisfaction and attain the level of self-actualization. While success is measured by others, satisfaction comes from within by our own assessment which is more important for self-actualization. The Government has to act as an enabler/facilitator by evolving the policy for **Institution Building** so that the real effectiveness can be realized by all of us.

It is not out of place to mention here that India is the largest democratic nation in the world with a population of 1.37 billion. We are ranked 100th on the Global Prosperity Index among the 149 countries showing a four-rank improvement from the previous year according to London based Legatum institute report released in November 2017. In the process it is catching up with China which ranks 90th in the Prosperity Index.

It is expedient for all of us (both individually as well as collectively) to take a pledge to involve ourselves in building the organization/Institution to ensure a better tomorrow for our youth by taking individual and Social responsibility. It is a matter of our mind over matter.

Individual Responsibility: One may make a **'Mountain out of a mole-hill'** as the tolerance level may vary from person to person according to their perceptions. Some may make tall claims while others may not make a mention about what all good things they did for individuals or for Society. It is quite possible that the former may be doing service unwillingly, out of compulsions or may do for publicity so that others may talk or think great about them. The latter kind of people on the other hand, may derive pleasure in helping others and consider the same as an opportunity or a boon rather than a bane. We must understand that it is all in the minds of the people how they perceive. After all **'Winners have dreams and Losers have only Schemes' as the Winners see the gains for everyone whereas losers see the pains for themselves as they cannot think beyond themselves.** To put it mildly, we must accept that the mental tiredness takes a heavier toll than the physical stress and fatigue on any individual. Unless and until a person becomes mentally tired s/he never gives up any task on hand however physically challenged s/he may be.

One can derive the real pleasure of serving and uplifting the family if s/he renders the unconditional support without any expectations. Talking or mentioning about our own (so called) good deeds reveals our expectation from others thereby loses its sanctity. The next generation can be built and groomed well, if we enable them to acquire higher education in their desired fields and teach them its importance to climb the pinnacle of success in life. One's real investment in life is not only providing higher education to the children but also inculcating to them the importance of culture & traditions and the art of blending the same with modernity. Similarly, taking care of his/her old aged parents, keeping them mentally happy, giving them solace by bestowing the best possible physical comforts, spending few hours with them daily and talking about their good old days/deeds are the real excellent ways of expressing his/her gratification and reciprocation of his/her love and affection to them.

Social Responsibility: It is a paradox that the adversity of poverty and missionaries of charities co-exist worldwide. Although there is no dearth of benevolence in the society, we are unable to ensure that the aid and funds that we receive from different organizations (NGOs) reach the concerned affected individuals without any pilferage because of involvement of many middlemen. When India, Indonesia and many other South Asian countries were affected by the catastrophic effect of Tsunami in December 2004, millions of $s poured in as donations and aids from all over the world but there was no fool-proof mechanism to ensure that it disseminated down to the needy ones in time barring few fortunate ones.

Citizens' charter and Right to Information Act 2005 (RTI Act 2005): It is worth mentioning here that the basic five principles involved in citizens' charter – (1) transparency, (2) accountability of all from top to bottom, (3) availability of adequate information, (4) providing quality services with commitment for continual improvement and (5) effective public grievance redress mechanism have been adequately addressed by the enactment of Right To Information (RTI) Act 2005 which remove the doubts and public grievances to a great extent.

Government Policy: We all know, for the last few years Government is making deductions towards education cess which is presently @4% of the income-tax from all. No doubt the intentions are good and well envisaged, but mere collection is not sufficient. They must ensure that concrete schemes are made and implemented so that the economically poorer (who are mostly in rural India) are the beneficiaries of such novel schemes. They should enable the poorer children to get not only the basic education but also higher/professional education by introducing merit-cum-means scholarships for the meritorious and deserving students among the poorer lot. Further, free hostel facilities, providing of books, uniforms etc. to such pupils for all levels of education cannot be overlooked. We have to initiate affirmative action to redress the effects of past discrimination with respect to caste, creed and sex by devising plans and promoting policies whereby only merit and means are considered as the criteria for giving education and employment so that qualitative students come out of the elite educational institutes to serve the corporate world and society.

Steps ahead: The emergence of many non-profit UGC recognized private Universities apart from the affiliated foreign Universities have enhanced the scope of many students in pursuing higher education/professional studies in the field of their choices at reasonable cost without going abroad. The introduction of single-girl child Scholarship by the Government in the year 2005–06 for post-graduate education is a step in the right direction for uplifting the girls students. Similarly, the government may envisage a plan for development of educational institutions (primary, secondary and higher) all over the country – both in urban and rural areas – by adopting the following scheme, if found appealing.

Rural vs. Urban: We must remember that our country's roots are based only at our rural India as 70% of our population is still in the villages and is agro-based. Therefore our priority has to be to uplift of our rural India which means uplifting our nation and economic growth. But the benefits do not reach them fully as of now nor do they get the desired opportunity and exposure for growth. Under the circumstances, we need to find ways and means to develop them without any extra cost and effort. The best method is to ensure more funds reach the educational institutes in rural areas so that they can emulate the prevailing best institutes in urban areas. The former Chief Minister of Tamil Nadu Shri. Kamaraj emphasized that the children should not travel more than one kilometre to get their basic and secondary education. In other words, Government should ensure that for every one kilometre there is a school of high standard (duly accredited by the concerned bodies to ensure quality education) so that every child can get proper education at primary and secondary levels. Similarly for every 20–30 kilometre there should be institutes providing higher education (including professional studies)-thereby, we can have high quality youth in our country who can fulfil our Country's dreams by meeting our **Vision and Mission.**

Corporate Social Responsibility: There is a mention of **CSR** in every annual Report of the private Sectors. To have the desired effect in the real sense for uplifting the poor, the private sectors should contribute in establishing premier educational institutions/ universities all over the country without having any profit motive where only meritorious students from the poor can be given the due priority. Tax exemptions may be given by the Government to the private sectors in respect of the amount spent on building such premier educational institutes/universities to give encouragement for their contributions towards the same. This will go a long way in raising our nation to a predominant level.

Our new vistas for the futuristic India are no doubt surmountable. Let our hunt be on in identifying and grooming the best talents in our nation by providing all necessary assistance/infrastructures to them by developing the best basic and professional educational institutes through funds generated by aforesaid means.

Our Government of India in keeping with its reform agenda has established **NITI (National Institution for Transforming India) Aayog** in the year 2015 by replacing the **Planning Commission.** Its vision is very clear as **NITI Aayog** is developing itself as a state of the art Resource centre, with the necessary resources, skills and knowledge which would enable it to act with speed, promote research and innovation, plan and provide strategic policies for the Government and deal with contingent issues for effective results. Digital India, Medical Education reform and agricultural reform are part of the initiatives and action plan to name a few which would surely raise our nation to a higher pedestal.

It is laudable that Government is seriously contemplating to make it compulsory for the medical students to serve the rural India at least for a minimum period of one year as part of their curriculum before awarding the degrees to them. This will definitely benefit both the students and the people who are residing in remote villages where proper medical facilities are not available. It will benefit the young Doctors to have more exposure to different kind of ailments faced by illiterate and poor people in rural areas. The Doctors while serving such people may bring about the necessary awareness to them who otherwise have no means to know about the ill-effects of various diseases caused by **HIV, TB, Dengue, Tape-Worm, Swine-Flu etc.** After all, **'Health is Wealth'** and the Quality of Life in the villages can be improved only by constructing hospitals equipped with modern facilities. By having young and experienced Doctors (who have exposure to the latest technology) serving in rural areas we can enhance the Quality of Life there.

The development in the areas of transport and communication together with the emergence of internet connections have made both urban and rural people to feel that they are no more distanced from each other however far they may be. It would not surprise anyone, if we turn out to be a **'Supersonic Nation' by the year 2020 in all respects and thereby fulfil the dream and Vision of our Hon'ble Late President Dr. APJ Abdul Kalam** who had mentioned in his biography, **'our birth may be an incident but our death should be the history.'** It only means that we should perform something with passion to emulate others so that the home, society, state and nation should talk about us and remember us forever. Let us get inspired by his words. After all, winners don't do different things; they do things differently, isn't it?

Chapter-16

Teacher vs. Mentor

- *A Teacher takes responsibility of your growth.*
- *A Mentor makes you responsible for your growth.*

- *A Teacher gives you things you do not have and require.*
- *A Mentor takes away things you have and do not require.*

- *A Teacher answers your questions.*
- *A Mentor questions your answers.*

- *A Teacher helps you get out of the maze.*
- *A Mentor destroys the maze.*

- *A Teacher requires obedience and discipline from the pupil.*
- *A Mentor requires trust and humility from the pupil.*

- *A Teacher clothes you and prepares you for the outer journey.*
- *A Mentor strips you naked and prepares you for the inner journey.*

- *A Teacher is a guide on the path.*
- *A Mentor is a pointer to the way.*

- *A Teacher sends you on the road to success.*
- *A Mentor sends you on the road to freedom.*

- *A Teacher explains the world and its nature to you.*
- *A Mentor explains yourself and your nature to you.*

- *A Teacher makes you understand how to move about in the world.*
- *A Mentor shows you where you stand in relation to the world.*

- *A Teacher gives you knowledge and boosts your ego.*
- *A Mentor takes away your knowledge and punctures your ego.*

- *A Teacher instructs you.*
- *A Mentor constructs you.*

- *A Teacher sharpens your mind.*
- *A Mentor opens your mind.*

- *A Teacher shows you the way to prosperity.*
- *A Mentor shows the way to serenity.*

- *A Teacher reaches your mind.*
- *A Mentor touches your spirit.*

- *A Teacher gives you knowledge.*
- *A Mentor bestows Wisdom to you.*

- *A Teacher gives you maturity.*
- *A Mentor returns you to innocence.*

- *A Teacher instructs you on how to solve problems.*
- *A Mentor shows you how to resolve issues.*

- *A Teacher is a systematic thinker.*
- *A Mentor is a lateral thinker.*

- ❖ *A Teacher will punish you with a stick.*
- ❖ *A Mentor will punish you with compassion.*

- ❖ *A Teacher is to pupil what a father is to son.*
- ❖ *A Mentor is to pupil what mother is to her child.*

- ❖ *One can always find a Teacher.*
- ❖ *But a Mentor has to find and accept you.*

- ❖ *A Teacher leads you by the hand.*
- ❖ *A Mentor leads you by example.*

- ❖ *When a Teacher finishes with you, you graduate.*
- ❖ *When a Mentor finishes with you, your life celebrates.*

- ❖ *When the course is over, you are thankful to the teacher.*
- ❖ *When the discourse is over, you are grateful to the Mentor. Let us honour both – the Teachers and Mentor in our Life.*

Mentor Vs Godfather

A Mentor is however not the Godfather. **"A mentor is someone who sees more talent and ability within you, than you see in yourself and helps bring it out of you" – Bob Proctor**

Mentor

- ❖ A Mentor is someone who teaches you by Example and Direction.

- ❖ A Mentor can work anywhere or may not work at all; but have skills and knowledge to impart. He/she may be your Boss or a Co-Worker.

- Mentor is described as an experienced and trusted advisor.
- Mentors are especially important in helping young people during their early stages of their career.

To be effective, a mentor:-

- Must be very skilled at acquiring and using power.
- Should be capable of building and utilizing relationships.
- Should have the influencing behaviour through example setting.
- Must develop mutually understood and accepted expectations in setting goals and objectives.
- Should closely observe performance by effective monitoring.
- Needs to have the ability to listen patiently and show empathy & trust.
- Should have the capability to analyse problems and show ways for resolving the same.
- Has to provide feedback to ensure continual improvement.

Qualities of Mentors

- They are superior performers in their own jobs.
- They become the role model.
- Their behaviour worth imitating.
- They are supportive and helpful, but avoid usurping the jobs of their subordinates or insist upon things being done exactly their way.

- They delegate and empower their subordinates while working towards their goals.

- They make subordinates self-beneficiaries/self-punishers for their actions and teach them to work under self-control.

Godfather

A Godfather:-

- Develops a special liking for someone and for his/her style.

- May be even connected to him/her in some way either by accident or by an incident which may be the cause for such liking.

- Helps his/her career from time to time and may protect him/her in difficult situations using his influence and position.

- May be working for the same Organization or the Agency the beneficiary serves.

- May not be his/her boss but in a much higher position in the same or different organization.

Education, Training and Development: Education usually means preparation for career and for life in general, which involves learning concepts, principles, problem-solving methods etc. and is provided by teachers to students at school and college levels. Whereas, training means preparation for a specific job or set of tasks and is imparted by organizations for employees/workforce to enhance their competencies. It involves learning and is designed to improve the performance of people doing jobs. On the other hand, Development is any learning activity which is directed towards future needs rather than present needs and is concerned more with career growth than immediate performance.

Thus Training and Development (T & D) refer to the imparting of specific skills, capabilities and knowledge to an employee. The need for

Training and Development is determined by employee's performance deficiency, computed as follows:

Training and Development Need = Standard Performance – Actual Performance

The deficiency is caused by lack of ability rather than lack of motivation to perform. Training process moulds the thinking of employees and leads to quality performance of employees. It is a continuous and never ending in nature along with the change in time and technology.

Training is essential for organisational development and success. It is beneficial for both employer and employees of an organization. Trained employees tend to stay with the organization as they become more efficient, confident and versatile in their operations.

Purpose of training: The aim of training is to help the organization to achieve its purpose by adding value to its key resource – the people it employs. The objectives of training the workforce are as follows:-

1. To increase productivity and quality. Well trained employees show both quantity and quality of performance. Training of employees ensures that there is less wastage of time, money and resources.

2. To improve profitability.

3. To promote versatility and adaptability to new methods.

4. To reduce the number of accidents by enhancing the competencies of workforce operating the machines, especially when new equipment or techniques are introduced.

5. To ensure availability of skills and pool of talents for organizational development and to increase scope for career advancement for individuals.

Training is given on the following four basic grounds:

1. Induction training is given for new candidates who join an organisation. This training familiarises them with the organizational mission, vision, rules & regulations and the working conditions.

2. The existing employees are trained to refresh and enhance their knowledge and skills at regular intervals.

3. If any updation and amendments take place in technology, training is given to cope up with those changes. For instance, employees are trained for use of new equipment with improved technology and for adopting new work methods.

4. When promotions and career growth become important, training is imparted to such employees so that they are equipped and prepared to take responsibilities of the higher level job.

Advantages of training: Training is an investment with a promise of better returns in future. The advantages of training people in an organization are as follows:-

1. Improves job knowledge, skills at all levels of the organization.

2. Improves the morale of the workforce as trained employees get more job security and job satisfaction.

3. Helps people identify themselves with the organizational goals.

4. Improves the relationship between employees and employer.

5. A well trained employee will be well acquainted with the job and therefore will need less supervision. Thus there will be less wastage of time and efforts.

6. Aids in development for promotion within the organization as employees acquire skills and efficiency through training. They become an asset for the organisation.

7. Aids in developing leadership skills, loyalty, motivation and positive attitudes of employees.

8. Reduces outside consulting costs with the availability of experienced and trained workforce within the organization.

Words of caution: We need to be cautious while sending people for training so as to ensure its effectiveness. We have to identify and impart need based training for employees to ensure that there is immediate scope for application of their new skills in the organization. Otherwise, such employees look for new opportunities/avenues outside after acquiring new skills. In the process, the organizations who spend huge amount on the training would be the loser if such people leave them on acquiring new skills. We need to measure the effectiveness of training programme by analysing the productivity, profitability and the reports of accidents. Further, while sending people for training we have to ensure that their present work is not affected in anyway, when they are away from their jobs for training purpose.

Feedbacks have to be obtained both from the trainer and the trainees to measure the effectiveness of any training programme and to assess whether the concerned individuals have acquired the required level of competencies after undergoing the training.

Chapter-17

Thoughtful Thoughts

1. THE QUALITY OF SERVICE AND PRODUCTIVITY OF EACH PERSON SHALL BE MADE EQUAL BY EFFECTVE AND PROPER UTILISATION OF HIS/HER AVAILABLE RESOURCES.

2. FOR QUALITY –

   DO WHAT IS RIGHT AND WRITE WHAT YOU DO.

   DO RIGHT THING AT THE RIGHT TIME IN THE FIRST TIME AND EVERY TIME.

   Measure, monitor and review to maintain quality and to ensure continual improvement.

3. MORE WE KNOW ABOUT ANY SUBJECT LESS WE FEEL LEARNT AND LESS WE LEARN ABOUT THE SAME, MORE WE FEEL KNOW ABOUT IT.

4. PAST HAS BECOME HISTORY; FUTURE IS ALWAYS A MYSTERY; ONLY OUR PRESNT IS OUR TRUE GIFT. SO LET US FOCUS OUR ATTENTION ON OUR PRESENT TASKS WHICH WILL ENSURE A BETTER FUTURE IF IT IS HANDLED EFFECTIVELY.

5. **DEFINITION OF A POLITICIAN:-**

   a) ONE WHO MAKES EFFECTIVE UTILISATION OF THE PRESENT SITUATION TO THE BENEFIT OF ALL PERSONS/ORGANISATION/AND NATION. EXAMPLE: FREEDOM FIGHTERS.

- **b)** ONE WHO MAKES THE BEST USE OF THE CURRENT SITUATION/POSITION TO HIS OWN BENEFITS. EXAMPLE: PRESENT POLITICIANS.

- **c)** ONE WHO PUSHES OTHERS TO A PLACE IN SUCH A WAY THAT THEY ACTUALLY LOOK FORWARD/LONG FOR THE SAME. EXAMPLE: FUTURE GENERATION.

6. ONE WILL GET MORE AND MORE POWERS AS LONG AS HE IS NOT MISUSING THE EXISTING POWERS.

7. DEVELOPING A LIKING FOR WHAT YOU DO RATHER THAN DOING WHAT YOU LIKE WILL ALWAYS ENSURE CONTENTMENT IN LIFE.

8. ONE SHOULD BE THOUGH CONTENTED ALWAYS WITH WHAT S/HE HAS/IS, S/HE SHOULD NEVER BE COMPLACENT IN ORDER TO HAVE A CONSISTENT GROWTH IN LIFE.

9. IN DECISION MAKING PROCESS, WE HAVE TO DRAW A LINE BETWEEN ETHICS AND INSTINCT AND BETWEEN HEART AND MIND TO MAKE THE SAME EFFECTIVE.

10. OUR DECISIONS WILL ALWAYS PROVE TO BE CORRECT SO LONG WE DO NOT WORK AGAINST OUR CONSCIENCE.

11. SO LONG THERE IS NO CONFLICT IN OUR VALUE SYSTEM, DECISION MAKING IS EASIER AND NO TIME AND ENERGY IS LOST.

12. TO LEAD A MEANINGFUL LIFE, ONE HAS TO GO FOR INTRINSIC VALUES RATHER THAN MATERIALISTIC BENEFITS.

13. IF YOU CANNOT EXCEL WITH YOUR TALENT, TRIUMPH IT WITH HARD WORK.

14. THOSE WHO DEAL WELL WITH PEOPLE CAN LEAD THEM WELL TOO.

15. WE NEED A BREAK TO HAVE A BREAK-THROUH AND TO AVERT TOTAL BREAK-DOWN.

16. JUST ENOUGH TO GO BY IS NOT ENOUGH TO GO AHEAD.

17. WE SHOULD DEVELOP INFINITE INTERESTS AND ENTHUSIASM IN THE FIRST HALF OF OUR LIFE AND IN THE LATER PART WE MUST SHOW MORE PATIENCE AND HUMILITY IN ORDER TO BE SUCCESSFUL THROUGHOUT.

18. QUALITY OF A PERSON CAN BE JUDGED NOT ONLY FROM HIS PRESENTATION SKILLS BUT ALSO THE MESSAGE S/HE CONVEYS THROUGH THE SAME AND THE MANNER IN WHICH S/HE DEMONSTRATES HER/HIS PERCEPTION/ CONVICTION BY HER/HIS ACTION.

19. FROM OUR EXPERIENCE WE MAY REALISE THAT EVEN TRUTH FAILS TO WIN AT TIMES, BUT IT ALWAYS PREVAILS.

20. COURAGE IS NEITHER THE ART/SKILL OF HIDING ONE'S COWARDLINESS NOR THE ABSENCE OF FEAR; BUT ACTUALLY OVERCOMING THE FEAR.

21. IN THIS IMPERFECT WORLD, EACH ONE OF US WISHES TO SHOW THAT HE OR SHE IS THE MOST PERFECT PERSON. UNLESS WE ALL BECOME PERFECT WE CANNOT MAKE THE WORLD PERFECT.

22. IT IS A PARADOX THAT WHEN YOU HAVE CONFIDENCE IN YOU/YOUR ACTIONS OTHERS DO NOT REPOSE CONFIDENCE IN YOU AND BY THAT TIME YOU EARN THEIR CONFIDENCE YOU WOULD HAVE LOST CONFIDENCE IN YOURSELVES.

23. WHEN YOU HAVE THE DESIRE AND ENERGY TO PERFORM YOU MAY NOT GET THE OPPORTUNITY AND WHEN YOU GET THE OPPORTUNITY TO SHOW YOUR EXCELLENCE YOU FEEL YOU HARDLY POSSESS ANY ENERGY/DESIRE/SKILL TO EXCEL. SO, AVAIL THE OPPORTUNITIES THAT COMES IN YOUR WAY RATHER THAN AVOIDING THE SAME BY CONSIDERING AS A THREAT.

24. LIFE IS A PILGRIMAGE.

    WE SHOULD HAVE A MISSION EVERYDAY.

    THOUGH WE ALL HAVE AN AMBITION, WE SHOULD HAVE A DISTANT AND DISTINCT VISION.

25. WE SHOULD NOT BE WORRIED ABOUT ANYTHING, THOUGH WE SHOULD BE CONCERNED ABOUT EVERYTHING.

26. NEVER EVER CRITICISE A PERSON OR HIS/HER ACTS; INSTEAD, APPRECIATE HIS/HER PROBLEM. SHOW EMPATHY RATHER THAN SHOWING SYMPATHY OR RIDICULING HIM/HER TO GET THE BEST OUT OF HIM/HER.

27. LET OTHERS USE US AS LONG AS IT IS BENEFICIAL TO EVERYBODY. BUT, LET NOT OTHERS USE US FOR THEIR OWN VESTED INTERESTS. LET US ENSURE WE ARE NEITHER ABUSED OR MISUSED BUT ARE PROPERLY USED.

28. LIFE IS A GIFT GIVEN BY GOD. IT IS UPTO THE INDIVIDUALS WHETHER TO EFFECTIVELY USE THE SAME FOR EVERYONE'S BENEFITS RATHER THAN WASTING IT.

29. LOSS OF TIME MAY BE APPRECIATED WHICH ARE BEYOND OUR CONTROL (EXTERNAL FACTORS), BUT WASTAGE OF TIME CANNOT BE TOLERASTED AS THEY ARE WITHIN OUR CONTROL (INTERNAL FACTORS).

30. LIFE HAS TO BE EXPERIENCED OR ENJOYED AND THERE IS NO OTHER OPTION EXISTS.

31. OUR MIND IS LIKE A PARACHUTE. IT WORKS ONLY WHEN IT IS OPEN.

32. GREAT MEN THINK ALIKE AND FOOLS SELDOM DIFFER. WHILE GREAT MEN THINK FOR A CAUSE, FOOLS ARE THE CAUSE FOR THINKING.

33. THINKING OF PROBLEM RATHER THAN THE SOLUTION IS ALWAYS A PROBLEM.

34. ANYTHING IN EXCESS IS BAD, EXCEPT KNOWLEDGE AND SHARING OF THE SAME WITH OTHERS.

35. IT IS TOO BAD TO BE TOO GOOD AND IT IS NOT ALWAYS GOOD TO BE TOO BAD.

36. WE BECOME TIRED ONLY WHEN OUR MIND BECOMES TIRED; WE REMAIN FRESH AS LONG AS OUR MIND REMAINS FRESH.

37. WE HAVE TO HAVE BELIEF IN OURSELVES AS WELL AS ON GOD, IF WE WANT TO LEAD A SUCCESSFUL LIFE THROUGHOUT.

38. A PERSON'S IMPORTANCE IS REALISED ONLY WHEN HIS PRESENCE OR ABSENCE BECOMES CONSPICUOUS. BY HIS GOOD DEEDS.

39. THE IMPORTANCE OF ANYTHING IS REALISED ONLY WHEN IT IS NOT DONE.

40. ONE'S REAL QUALITIES BECOME EVIDENT ONLY, WHEN ALL ODDS ARE TOTALLY AGAINST HIM/HER.

41. a. THE **SIX** MOST IMPORTANT WORDS ONE SHOULD REMEMBER ALWAYS ARE, **"I ADMIT I DID A MISTAKE."**

b. THE **FIVE** MOST IMPORTANT WORDS TO BE USED ARE, **"YOU DID A GOOD JOB."**

c. THE **FOUR** MOST IMPORTANT WORDS WE SHOULD OFTEN USE ARE, **"WHAT IS YOUR OPINION?"**

d. THE **THREE** MOST IMPORTANT WORDS WE SHOULD USE ARE **"WILL YOU PLEASE…"**

e. THE **TWO MOST** IMPORTANT WORDS TO BE USED ARE, **"THANK YOU."**

f. THE **MOST** IMPORTANT WORD WE SHOULD OFTEN BUT SELDOM USE IS, **"WE."**

g. THE **LEAST** IMPORTANT ONE LETTER WORD BUT MOSTLY USED BY US IS, **"I."**

42. THERE IS SO MUCH GOOD IN THE WORST OF US AND SO MUCH BAD IN THE BEST OF US WHICH REMAIN IN STORE TO FIND FAULT IN THE REST OF US.

43. FUN THOUGHTS/MODERN DEFINITIONS:

- Most Loyal Employee: One who cannot get a job anywhere else.

- Exceptionally well Qualified: One who has made no major blunders yet.

- Socially Active: One who drinks in parties.

- Family active socially: Wife too drinks in parties.

- Quick Thinking: Offers plausible excuses.

- Careful Thinker: One who would not take any decision on any matter.

- Aggressive: Obnoxious.

- Most proud and arrogant person: Too short that he/she keeps his/her head high always while talking to his/her colleagues.

- Most brainy/studious person: wearing thick glasses.

- Good Strategist for difficult jobs: Never takes any responsibility but pass on the work to others to do it.

- Expresses themselves well: Speaks English well.

- Most popular and attractive person in the office: Always talks and laughs aloud.

- Great Presentation Skills: One who brags a lot and able to justify his/her actions logically.

- Meticulous attention to detail/Minimum Risk Taker: A nil picker.

- Has leadership Qualities: One who is tall or has a loud/deep voice.

- Most humble and obedient person: Too tall a person that he/she keeps his/her head down while talking with others.

- Exceptionally good judgment: Lucky always.

- Great sense of Humour: One who Knows and cracks a lot of dirty jokes.

- Career minder: Backstabber.

- Work is Top Priority: Too ugly to get a date.

- Independent Worker: Nobody knows what he/she does.

- Most serious and silent worker: who neither talks nor smiles to others.

- Great Team player: Never say 'No' to any team member.

- A true consultant: One who takes the subject you understand but makes it sounds confusing.

- Since light travels faster than sound, people look bright until you hear them speak.

44. WE HAVE TO RESIST OURSELVES FROM **ANGER** AS IT IS **JUST ONE** LETTER SHORT OF THE WORD **'DANGER'** WHICH IS DISASTROUS.

45. WE HAVE TO CHANGE OURSELVES INSTEAD OF TRYING TO CHANGE OTHERS.

46. FORGIVE THE PERSON BUT NOT FORGET THE INCIDENT, AS IT IS AN EXPERIENCE AND A LESSON TO PONDER WITH FOREVER IN YOUR FUTURE ENDEAVOR.

47. UNLESS YOU ARE HONEST TO YOURSELF AND IN YOUR THINKING, YOU CANNOT BE HONEST TO OTHERS.

48. AT LEAST EXPERIENCE YOU GET WHEN YOU AIM/ASPIRE FOR SOMETHING BIG.

49. WE LEARN A LESSON OR TWO FROM EACH EXPERIENCE WHICH GIVES CLARITY TO OUR THOUGHTS WHICH IS OUR ULTIMATE PLEASURE. THAT IS WHY IT IS SAID, EXPERIENCE IS THE BEST TEACHER.

50. LIFE MUST BE UNDERSTOOD BACKWARD: BUT IT MUST BE LIVED FORWARD.

51. WHEN WE GET HALF OF OUR AMBITION FULFILLED OUR PROBLEMS IN LIFE WOULD BECOME DOUBLE.

52. BE SINCERE IN YOUR EFFORTS AND LEAVE THE REST TO DESTINY.

53. MATURITY IS THE REFLECTION OF EXPERIENCE AND RATIONAL THINKING WHICH ENABLES US TO PERFORM CONSISTENTLY FOR CONTINUAL IMPROVEMENT.

54. IF WE FAIL TO PLAN, WE ARE PLANNING TO FAIL.

55. SITUATION DOES NOT DISTURB US. IT IS OUR VIEW OF THE SITUATION THAT DISTURBS US.

56. A HAPPY AND CONTENTED PERSON CONVERT THE HELL INTO HEAVEN AND A DIISSATISFIED PERSON WILL MAKE EVEN HEAVEN INTO HELL.

57. WHEN TRUE BLISS IS INEXPENSIVE, WHY PEOPLE SPEND SO MUCH MONEY FOR/IN SEARCH OF TEMPORARY HAPPINESS.

58. SALVATION DOES NOT LEAD A PERSON TO HEAVEN BUT BRING HEAVEN INTO ONESELF.

59. OPPORTUNITIES ARE EQUAL FOR ALL. BUT THE DIFFRENCE IS, POSITIVE PERSON GIVES RESULTS AND NEGATIVE PERSON GIVES REASONS/EXCUSES.

60. SUBMISSIVE PERSONS BLAME THEMSELVES; AGGRESSIVE PERSONS BLAME OTHERS;

ASSERTIVE PERSONS NEITHER BLAME THEMSELVES NOR OTHERS. BUT THEY FIX THE PROBLEM.

61. BLAMING OTHERS MEANS LACK OF EDUCATION; BLAMING ONESELF MEANS EDUCATION HAS JUST COMMENCED;

NEITHER BLAMING OTHERS NOR ONESELF MEANS EDUCTION IS COMPLETE.

62. FOUR THINGS WE CANNOT RECOVER:

    i.   The stone after the throw in an ocean,

    ii. The word after it is said or mailed,

    iii. Occasion after the loss,

    iv. The time after it is gone.

63. IN THIS WORLD, NOTHING IS FREE. EITHER IT IS PRE-PAID OR POST-PAID. SO, IF WE WANT TO RECEIVE, WE NEED TO LEARN TO GIVE FIRST...MAYBE WE WILL END WITH OUR HANDS EMPTY, BUT OUR HEARTS WILL BE FILLED WITH LOVE. AND THOSE WHO LOVE LIFE, HAVE THAT FEELING MARKED IN THEIR HEARTS...

64. YOU RETIRE WHEN PEOPLE ASK WHY-RATHER THAN WHY NOT?

PART - II

Case Study

The Young Gun vs. The Old One
By Prof. Nischal Mahajan

"Age is an issue of mind over matter. If you don't mind it doesn't matter" Mark Twain had famously said.

9:10 p.m., Friday. Shreya was sorting out the papers on her desk and preparing to leave for home. She usually left office by seven, to drive down to her home located at a comfortable distance of two kilometres. She always looked forward to reaching home and spending quality evening time with her four-year-old son.

As Shreya picked up her car keys and made her way to the exit door, she felt that the thoughts in her mind were racing ahead of her in an uncontrolled fashion. Walking down the second floor steps from the office towards her car, she was unmindful of the light evening breeze that was blowing across her face. She was walking and rubbing the point between her eyebrows, as if coaxing a thought out.

Shreya, a dynamic and charismatic MBA graduate from one of the premier B-schools, had been recently promoted to the post of Regional Head. She had been working with her current organisation, a French multinational in the service industry, since seven years, and she had joined as Key Account Manager. Through focus on her work, she had climbed up the career ladder smoothly and steadily, while seamlessly adapting to her current role of Regional Head.

Her thoughts went back to the evening's happening, when one of the star performers in her team, Kalpana (Area Manager – Client relations), had put down her papers, owing to personal reasons.

Shreya felt that since she had recently become a mother, she was probably unable to balance her personal and professional lives. This also probably explained why counselling had failed to persuade her from staying at the job.

She was now thinking that amidst the strong competition and global recession, when the only way for survival was retention of the existing clients, the unexpected resignation from her star CRM team member has acted as a major dampener in her eventual quest for target achievement in her region. With these thoughts in her mind, Shreya focused on playing with her son, who was now trying to draw her attention towards him. She decided that it would be best to deal with the issue the following day.

The next morning, when Shreya was sitting in her office, analysing how 80 per cent of revenues for the region came from the repeat business of existing clients, she realized that her clients had now been left without a dedicated resource to service them. The manager-customer relationship, which is of paramount importance in service organization, was missing and she wondered: What if the clients are offered better technology? What if they are offered reduced commercials? What if they are offered better value propositions, attractive deals etc.? Will they come back to us? Will they approach us and give us the first right of refusal? – All uncertain scenarios.

Shreya was facing an immense amount of pressure from the top management to fill in the vacant position. She needed a strong resource, someone who was mature and could fill in the vacancy immediately. More importantly, someone who could strike a rapport with clients instantaneously. Aggressive hunting for the right candidate began. Job descriptions were shared with leading consultants. CVs started pouring in but no suitable candidate was found.

Due to the fact that it had been two months since the position first fell vacant during which time most clients had remained unattended, the pressure from the top management was mounting. Even her CEO, Rajesh Sood, expressed his grave concern against the backdrop of the current recessionary environment and the seriousness of retention of existing customers.

As luck would have it, her National sales Head, Alok Sharma, called her up and stated that there was an old resource, Anant, who had been with the company a few years back. Alok had met him recently, and in the course of the discussion, he had expressed his desire to apply for the opening. He wanted the job desperately and also knew the systems well. After Shreya finished the conversation with Alok, she stretched back in her chair, all this while looking at the ceiling and feeling apprehensive about filling the post. She had pointed out in no uncertain terms to Alok that the said gentleman was 42 years of age whereas the average age of her branch was 27 years.

The top management seemed convinced that he was capable of taking up the role and could assist the Regional Head in venturing into new territories. The biggest strength was his comfort level and knowledge about the systems; the fact was that he could be productive from day one. Alok vividly recollected that Anant Ghanshyam, the man in question, would come to work early, work through the lunch hour and even on the weekends. But Shreya was fighting her own battle in her mind: whether she should go ahead with Anant's appointment, or if she should look for someone younger who had one or two years of experience.

Shreya, with over a decade of work experience behind her, had never experienced such a situation before. She had been a brilliant performer ever since she had joined the organisation. She had faced and surmounted many challenges while achieving her targets on a consistent basis, thus growing to her current role where she was leading a staff of 25 people. However at this challenge, she did not know what to do. Also crossing her mind was the thought of how effectively he would fit into the team and adapt to the culture that she had painstakingly built over the past four years.

The age-old Indian ethos of respecting one's elders kept coming back to her. How do you legitimately tell someone who is older than you what to do? Shreya was very sceptical. "My subordinate would be 12 years older than me!" she exclaimed out loud, he looked so elderly and he may have a very rigid thought process. Would he be able to adjust with the young team and would he be open to change? Although Shreya was very affable with her team members, at times she did lose her temper, more specifically on account of inefficiencies and weak achievement of potential performers. Unsurprisingly, she was worried if he would be able to bear that.

Another thought that crossed her mind was with regard to new employee orientation. Companies operating in highly competitive industries recognized the value of this process. She knew that a new employee would require several weeks or even months of training to become familiar with the company, its products, culture, policies and even the competition. She knew that unlike the older employee who had worked in the organisation previously and knew the systems well, the new employee would not be productive from day one. This may lead to a further loss of business in the current downturn.

On the other hand, the two generations' divergent work styles and perceptions of each other could create work challenges. Recalling her OB lectures during the first year of her MBA curriculum, she was reliving the fact that older workers preferred meeting regularly to discuss projects and goals, whereas younger employees were more likely to hand their team members a project and let them run with it.

What, if she waited and hired a younger resource, who had an open and flexible approach, who could think ahead of the times? Why could they not try to mould him/her as per the organisation's requirements?

Why could they not try to align the new resource strategically with the team and let him/her learn on the job? Moreover, there was no risk of the new recruit being viewed as deadweight by the existing younger employee within the team.

In India Inc. the 'younger boss-older employee' facet of working life is becoming more common as the number of over-55 workers increases. Keeping in mind this prevailing trend, what should Shreya next step be?

The Author's Viewpoints on the above Case Study: Generation '(E) X' and Generation 'Y (oung)'

The given case is a very interesting story that resonates the prevalence of the gap between Generation '(E) X' and Generation 'Y(oung)' and their divergent work styles in the contemporary corporate world. I would like to analyze the case on two accounts – first from the organization's perspective and then from Shreya's point of view.

The stiff competition and the recent global recession have put stress on the importance of retaining the existing clients who contribute 80 percent of the revenue in the region for the French multinational company. The manager-customer relationship is imperative for obvious reasons. The void created by the resignation of the star performer, Kalpana (from CRM) needs immediate attention as 2 months have already passed since she left. If a company engaged in the service industry fails to attend to its clients, there will always be a threat of losing them to competitors.

Under the circumstances, if no suitable candidate can be found, it would be prudent to give a chance to Anant Ghanshyam who had worked with them earlier and was quite familiar with the systems. Since the National Sales Head, Alok Sharma, has referred him, Anant's credibility cannot be doubted. However, efforts should be made to find out why Anant is desperate to join the company again. It may be because, firstly Alok felt that he would fit into the prevailing circumstances; or secondly, because Anant has problem with the present company, or thirdly because of both the reasons and Alok might be of the view that it would be mutually beneficial. In either of three cases, one cannot compromise on the organization's goals and therefore individuals should play their role judiciously.

From the top management perspective, it is clear that by recruiting him again, they can not only find a replacement for Kalpana, but also get reasonable assistance from him for the Regional Head in venturing into new territories, because of his extensive knowledge about the prevailing system.

Another cardinal fact one cannot overlook is that Shreya would be handling an elderly employee, Anant, who would need to report to and assist her. The top management must obviously be clear that to build Gen next, one has to develop Gen 'Y' and for doing so, Gen '(E) X' plays a decisive role.

We must remember Franklin D. Roosevelt's words, "We cannot always build the future for our youth, but we can build our youth for the future." Thus, having an appropriate blend of young and experienced employees will always be beneficial for any organization as the former exhibit a great deal of enthusiasm and have a relatively short-term view of their jobs, while the latter are more focused on long-term goals and generally believe in their qualities of patience, caution and establishing long term working relationships.

Keeping the above aspects in mind, Shreya should not be averse to the suggestion made by Alok for recruiting Anant Ghanshyam again (maybe as a stop-gap arrangement). In case she rejects his proposal, there is no guarantee that she will find a more suitable person. Any new employee may need months of training to get acclimatized with the company. The best course of action would be to recruit Anant on a contractual basis for a period of one year by stipulating his KRAs to be outlined like the following:

- 70 to 80 per cent KRAs should focus on retaining existing customers by not only meeting their requirements but also by getting repeat orders from them.

- The remaining 20 to 30 per cent KRAs would be for venturing into new territories.

During this one year contract period, she should not interfere in his day-to-day activities. She may monitor his progress through monthly review meeting so that both may feel comfortable with each other. She needs to adopt the situational leadership style so that they can facilitate each other in carrying out their responsibilities. Should Anant fulfil his KRAs after one year, he may be rewarded by promoting him as the Senior Manager Customer Relationship. Simultaneously, she may appoint another junior to be groomed by Anant and her to take care of the existing clients. Slowly Anant may become more involved in expanding the territorial business. On the other hand, if Anant fails to meet the KRAs in the one year period, then his contract should be terminated on the date of its expiry. In this case, the process of finding a suitable young person as a permanent replacement for Kalpana should be quietly commenced slightly in advance.

Epilogue

As mentioned in the **'Prologue,'** the emergence of **Human Resource Department (HRD)** actually took place quite late in Indian context, when organizations started focusing towards. **'Training & Development (T & D)'** of workforce to enhance their competencies and productivity. Great strides have been made in the last 3 decades in that direction which is quite noticeable. HR Managers have now become the cornerstone of any growing organization which has a flatter structure. However in this digital era, we need to appreciate that change is inevitable; we therefore need to change along with the time and technology to adapt ourselves to changing situations to make progress in this competitive business environment.

Currently E-commerce, E-wallet, smart phones, smart cards and online payments are the buzzwords commonly used in our day to day dealings/transactions with people. Even driver-less operation of cars and metro rail are being experienced now which could not be imagined a decade ago. The role of Human Resources (HR) is also changing with the emergence of digital world in the recent past. HR leaders can no longer continue to operate according to old paradigms as rapid change is not limited to technology alone, but encompasses society and demographics as well. They must now embrace new innovative ways in handling companies and the available talents. No wonder flexi times, sabbatical leave and working from home have been encouraged by companies to accommodate and retain the talented workforce. Further, online training and even examinations modules have also been developed to give wider scope for advancement.

It is abundantly clear that technology is advancing at an unprecedented pace, Technologies/Algorithms such as artificial intelligence (AI), Machine Learning (ML), robotics, sensors, mobile platforms and social collaboration systems have revolutionized our style of life – the way we live, work and communicate-we need to accept that everything is really accelerating at an exponential pace. While individuals adapt to the changing technology quickly, businesses and organizations move at a slower pace. The business practice of corporate planning, organizational structure, job-design, goal-setting and management were largely developed in the (first) industrial age and have now become out-dated. It is high time now that the companies must revise them to keep pace with/adapt to the technology and lifestyle changes. The implications of such changes are profound and this is where the HR plays a very crucial role in re-writing the rules and finding the organization of the future.

Today we have 4 to 5 generations of employees working under the same organization. We feel there is a generation change even if there is a difference of only 5 years unlike earlier times when we used to talk of generation gap only if there is an age difference of 15 to 20 years among employees. We therefore need to formulate and develop heterogeneous HR policies not only to respect but also to take care of diverse kind of employees (with respect to age, education, talent and gender).

The Chief Human Resource Officer (CHRO) should act as a business partner/manager to enable the organization to have the best of talent and opportunities for growth. We must appreciate that human capital is the intellectual property and intangible asset of any organization which needs to be nurtured and developed by the Human Resource Department; their intrinsic value is immeasurable and therefore cannot be reflected in the balance sheet of any company.

The main focus area of HR in future would therefore be for organizational knowledge and innovative ideas to stay ahead of the time not only to meet the demands of the customers but also to have an edge over the competitors.

Here we must also remember the importance of effective use of communication. No doubt with the advancement of telecommunication (4G and 5G etc.), multimedia and internet we are able to have an easy access with anyone staying at any part of the world in no time and therefore distance is no more a problem for communicating with people. But in the process, people who are staying nearby if not, in the same room have distanced themselves and the human touch is found missing which is not a healthy sign. Here also HR people can act as a conduit in bringing employees together by organizing sports activities, picnics, get-together etc. for their employees and families which would also bring about the much needed work-life balance.

We need to respond to the ways in which the millennia's world is changing. We cannot deny the significance of emotions, ethics and value system in human life in order to promote harmony in our society/organization. Emotional Intelligence (EI) is therefore as important as Artificial Intelligence (AI). Only adherence to ethics can take us closer to self-realisation/satisfaction, self-respect/discipline and self-compassion/control which in turn would improve our emotional health essential to a great extent for making decisions.

Despite having spiritual and cultural heritage, we rarely come across contemporary books of ethics that can serve as a practical or authentic life-guide. This is why many people lack self-confidence and live in a state of bewilderment.

So, the real challenging time ahead for HR people/other professionals and managers and in a way is also a great opportunity for them.

Hopefully, this book would prove to be a simple guide for People Management.

Notes:

www.ingramcontent.com/pod-product-compliance
Lightning Source LLC
Chambersburg PA
CBHW030940180526
45163CB00002B/647